AQA Physical Education

Second Edition

GCSE

Kirk Bizley

Nelson Thornes

First published in 2009 by Nelson Thornes Ltd
This edition published in 2013 by:
Nelson Thornes Ltd
Delta Place
27 Bath Road
CHELTENHAM
GL53 7TH
United Kingdom

13 14 15 16 17 / 10 9 8 7 6 5 4 3 2 1

A catalogue record for this book is available from the British Library

ISBN 978 1 4085 2230 1

Cover photograph: iStockphoto

Illustrations by David Russell Illustration and Rupert Besley

Page make-up by Wearset Ltd, Boldon, Tyne and Wear

Printed in China by 1010 Printing International Ltd

Acknowledgements

The author and the publisher would like to thank the following for permission to reproduce material:

Alamy: 3.2B (Stephen Shepherd), 5.1A (Angela Hampton Picture Library), 5.2B (Paul Doyle), 5.9B Eileen Langsley Gymnastics, 6.1B (Profimedia International s.r.o), 7.2A (Sally and Richard Greenhill), 7.3A (Adrian Sherratt), 7.3B (Sally and Richard Greenhill), 9.1A (The Photolibrary Wales), 10.3A (Roger Bamber), 10.4A (Mikael Utterström), 10.4B (Red Snapper), 13.1A (Hugh Threlfall), 13.1C (Jupiter Images/Banana Stock), 13.1D (Digital Vision), 13.1E (Jupiter Images/Thinkstock), 13.1F (Bobo), 13.2B (Jupiter Images/Pixland), 13.4A (Jupiter Images/Banana Stock); **Corbis**: 1.3B (Luo Xiaoguang/ Xinhua Press), 2.2B (Catherine Ivill/AMA), 3.1A (Pete Saloutos), 6.5A (Dan Forer/Beateworks), 12.1A (Alan Schein/Zefa), 12.3B (Tony Latham/LOOP Images); **Dame Kelly Holmes Legacy Trust**: 8.4B; **Dartfish**: 12.9A; **Flora London Marathon**: 4.2B; **Food Standards Agency**: 4.1A; **Fotolia**: 1.6B, 1.7A, 1.9B, 5.8A, 5.8B; **Getty Images**: 1.1B, 1.2A, 1.2B (AFP), 1.4A, 1.4B (AFP), 1.5B (WireImage/Jeff Fishbein), 1.7B, 1.9A (Man Utd), 2.1A (David Rogers – RFU), 2.1B, 2.3B, 2.5A (Sports Illustrated), 3.1B (Inti St Clair), 4.2A (AFP), 5.1B, 5.6B, 5.7B (AFP), C6, 6.1A (AFP), 6.2B, 6.3A, 6.6B (Tyler Stableford), 8.1B, 8.4A, 9.1B, 9.2B (AFP), 102A (Sports Illustrated), 10.3B (Axiom Photographic Agency), 11.1A, 11.1B, 11.2B (Sports Illustrated), 11.3A, 11.3B, 11.3C, 12.2A (AFP), 12.2B (AFP), 12.3A, 12.5A, 12.6A Alistair Berg), 12.6B, 12.8A (AFP), 13.3A (Paris Match), 13.5A; **Jim Wileman**: 7.2B; **Hawk-Eye**: 12.9B; **iStockphoto**: 1.3A, 1.8A, 1.8B, 2.2A, 2.4B, 2.7B, 3.2A, 4.1B, 5.4B, 5.7A, 5.9A, 6.5B, 6.5C, 6.6A, 10.2B, 13.1B, 13.2A, 13.2C, Exam section banner; **Library of Congress**: 11.2A; **PA Photos**: 12.4A (Nam Y Huh), 12.4B (Rui Vieira), 12.5B (Paulo Amorim), 12.7B (John Walton), 12.9C (Mike Egerton); **Rex Features**: 2.5B (Lehtikuva OY), 6.2A (Philip Brown), 12.B (Tony Kyriacou), 12.8B (NBCU Photobank); **Sport England**: 8.1A, 8.2A; **Sports Shots**: 8.2B; **Youth Sport Trust**: 8.3A, 8.3B (both Louise Roberts).

A special thanks to the staff and pupils at Downend School, Bristol for participating in our photo shoot.

Every effort has been made to trace the copyright holders but if any have been inadvertently overlooked the publisher will be pleased to make the necessary arrangements at the first opportunity.

Contents

Nelson Thornes

Nelson Thornes has worked hard to ensure this book and the accompanying online resources offer you the best support for your GCSE course.

These print and online resources together **unlock blended learning**; this means that the links between the activities in the book and the activities online blend together to maximise your understanding of a topic and help you achieve your potential.

These online resources are available on **kerboodle** which can be accessed via the internet at **www.kerboodle.com**, anytime, anywhere. If your school or college subscribes to **kerboodle** you will be provided with your own personal login details. Once logged in, access your course and locate the required activity.

For more information and help on how to use **kerboodle** visit **www.kerboodle.com**.

How to use this book

Objectives

Look for the list of **Learning Objectives** based on the requirements of this course so you can ensure you are covering the key points.

Study tip

Don't forget to look at the **Study tips** throughout the book as well as practise answering **Practice Questions**.

Visit **www.nelsonthornes.com/aqagcse** for more information.

Purpose of the qualification

This GCSE is primarily for you to be able to make full use of your expertise in the subject area of physical education to gain a GCSE qualification. This can not only go towards contributing toward your aim of achieving this GCSE, but could also start you on a career path in physical education and sport. It is just as valid as any other GCSE subject available, and it does have the added advantage of allowing you to gain up to 60 per cent of your total marks by actually performing as the assessed component for your practical work (Controlled Assessment).

What is covered in the qualification?

You will have to study a number of theory aspects which will form the basis of your knowledge to be able to answer questions set in the written examination, but these topics should also help you to become more competent in your assessed practical performance (Controlled Assessment). The theory you will be covering is designed specifically for you to be able to apply it to the other aspects of the course; from helping you to fully understand the body systems which contribute to physical performance, right through to helping you perform a different role such as that of an official.

What are the different qualifications?

Throughout the book you will you will see reference to the Short Course, Full Course and Double Award. In all qualifications, you can achieve up to 40 per cent of your total marks in written examinations (theory) and 60 per cent of your total marks through Controlled Assessment (practical coursework).

What do I need to learn?

Your teacher will be able to tell you which of the three qualifications you are taking. Throughout this book, each double-page spread of content is marked with appropriate tabs, telling you which qualification that specific content relates to. Look for your letter: **S** (Short Course), **F** (Full Course) and **D** (Double Award). The tabs can be found in the top-left hand corner of each double-page topic.

A *You can achieve up to 60 per cent of your total marks through Controlled Assessment (practical coursework)*

D F S	This section needs to be studied for all qualifications: Short Course, Full Course and Double Award.
D F	This section needs to be studied for Full Course and Double Award qualifications.
D	This section needs to be studied only for the Double Award.

Short Course (S)

If you are entered for this qualification, you will sit a 45-minute written examination paper (theory) covering Unit 1 of the specification. The written examination will require you to learn only some (not all – see *What do I need to learn?* on page 7) of the content contained in this book. Read the whole book and more widely to extend your knowledge though. You will have two practical assessments (Controlled Assessment) covering Unit 2 of the specification, which is described in Chapter 13 of this book.

Full Course (F)

If you are entered for this qualification, you will sit a 1 hour 30-minute written examination paper (theory) covering Unit 3 of the specification. The written examination will require you to learn most (not all – see *What do I need to learn?* on page 7) of the content contained in this book. Read the whole book and more widely to extend your knowledge though. You will have four practical assessments (Controlled Assessment) covering Unit 4 of the specification, which is described in Chapter 13 of this book.

Double Award (D)

If you are entered for this qualification, you will sit two 1 hour 30-minute written examination papers (theory) covering Units 3 and 5 of the specification. The written examination will require you to learn all of the content contained in this book (see *What do I need to learn?* on page 7). You will have eight practical assessments (Controlled Assessment) covering Units 4 and 6 of the specification, which is described in Chapter 13 of this book.

B *It is important that you find out from your teacher whether you have been entered for the Short Course, Full Course or Double Award*

1 The participant as an individual

Aims

✔ Be aware of the effects that ageing may have on the body and how these might affect the suitability for certain activities.

✔ Be aware of types of disabilities that exist and the ways in which the disabled can still be active participants.

✔ Be aware of the differences that exist between males and females and how this can affect participation.

✔ Be aware of how the culture in which someone lives or is brought up can influence levels of participation and choices of sports or activities.

✔ Be aware of the links between body type and how this might affect the suitability for particular activities.

✔ Consider the effects that various aspects of the environment may have upon levels of participation.

✔ Be aware of the factors of risk and challenge and their importance in physical activity.

✔ Consider the variety of activity levels and needs that exist.

✔ Be aware of the factors that affect the performers' and participants' ability to train.

This chapter focuses on the different aspects that affect and influence each individual – some are factors that the individual is able to control and some are not. Being aware of them is the first step, but being aware of the effects each can have is the next step.

There are considerable links between all these factors, so it is important that you consider them in relation to the fact that all people are individuals with different needs and the majority of factors will also apply to you as an individual.

Where there is some element of control or choice in the factor (such as risk and challenge, activity levels and training), being informed may help you to make some choices, but other factors cannot be altered and you may need to take these into account in your own individual participation.

1.1 Age

Age is one of those factors that we cannot do anything about as it is beyond our control, but being aware of the effects of ageing is important. This links to our **physiology** as well because there are various physical effects that ageing has on the body that are likely to effect the ways in which we are able to participate.

Physical activity and age

Our age directly affects our physical maturity and this in turn affects our suitability for certain activities for the following reasons:

- **Flexibility** may be quite high in our teens but tends to decrease with age. This can combine with a tendency to put on weight, which can also reduce flexibility.

A *Young gymnasts have greater levels of flexibility, which helps them perform better and score more highly*

- Strength decreases as we get older, but much younger people will not achieve maximal strength until they are fully grown, in their late teens or early twenties. This is why weight training is not recommended for certain age groups.
- Oxygen capacity reduces with age and the heart becomes less efficient. The arteries gradually lose their elasticity, increasing blood pressure and reducing blood flow.
- Skill levels can improve with age and experience, as well as improving as we grow and get stronger – a tall basketball player may find shooting skills easier than a short person.
- The older you get, the longer you take to recover from injuries, there is more chance of suffering from disorders or diseases, and there is a gradual build up of wear and tear on the body.

links

Find out more about the physical and mental demands of performance in Chapter 2 and health, fitness and a healthy active lifestyle in Chapter 5.

Being aware of these factors allows an individual to cope with them and take them into consideration. It is for this reason that nearly all top-level gymnasts **peak** in their mid-teens. Few, if any, go on to compete into their twenties.

Age divisions

One of the most basic ways that sport responds to the factor of age is to introduce age divisions into competitive sport. School sport is always organised within year groups and it is very unusual for this not to happen. Major sports organise competitions, championships and leagues around age but may allow some flexibility by arranging under-14, under-16 and under-18 events where it is possible for some players to play older competitors. The reason for this is that age does not always affect people in exactly the same way and some young people will physically mature quicker and be able to cope with older opponents. However, this is not so common in physical contact sports owing to the possible dangers of a physical mismatch.

B   *Laura Robson won the under-18 title at Wimbledon in 2008 when she was only 14*

1.2 Disability

Disability is an area where the social perception has been raised through policies of **inclusion** to ensure that all people are catered for.

Disability can be considered to exist in one of four categories:

- Physical
- Mental
- Permanent
- Temporary.

All of the above will affect an individual's ability to take part, but there are various ways in which these different disabilities can be catered for.

Sporting adaptations

All sports can be adapted to cater for either general or specific abilities. All governing bodies make efforts to make their sport accessible to all, as the following examples show:

- The Paralympics are held every four years immediately after the Olympic Games. In 2008 there were 20 different events, which ranged from athletics through to **equestrian** events and five-a-side and seven-a-side football. The event gets its name from the Parallel Olympics, which was first started in 1948 following the Second World War. Many other competitions are also organised by the IPC (International Paralympic Committee), which was founded in 1989 and is the international governing body of sports for athletes with a disability. They were responsible for the first Winter Paralympics in 1994 and encourage all sports authorities to provide competitions for disabled competitors in that sport.

A *Matt Stutzman of the United States competes in the Men's Individual Compound Archery at the London 2012 Paralympic Games*

Objectives

Consider the types of disability that exist.

Look at the ways in which disabled performers are able to be active participants.

Consider the measures taken to enable the disabled to participate as fully as possible.

Key terms

Inclusion: a policy that no one should experience barriers to learning as a result of their disability, heritage, gender, special educational need, ethnicity, social group, sexual orientation, race or culture.

Equestrian: relating to horseback riding or horseback riders.

links

There are links here to pages 10–11 and 18–19, as well as to the physical and mental demands of performance in Chapter 2. There will also be links to science in sport on pages 148–149.

- Adapted sports, such as wheelchair basketball, where the hoop heights are the same but some of the rules (such as travelling) are adapted.

- Adapted equipment, such as footballs used by the blind and visually impaired, where there are ball-bearings in small compartments within the ball so that it is audible and its movement can be tracked. Other adapted equipment, such as specially designed and adapted wheelchairs, are now available, not only for basketball and athletics (here each distance event has different types), but also for fishing, hockey, tennis, rugby, exercise, yoga and dance.

- Disability classifications exist for all activities relating to the particular physical demands of that sport. For instance, athletics uses a system of letters (T for track and F for field) and numbers, which identify the particular disability to make competition fair.

Activity

Choose one of the 20 sports featured in the Paralympics and find out all the disability classifications for one particular activity or event.

B *Blind runners have able-bodied runners who run next to them to guide them straight down the track. Here China's Jia Juntingxian (left) runs with her guide Xu Dongloin (right) during the Women's 200 metres T11 semifinal at the London 2012 Paralympic Games.*

Facilities

It is a legal requirement that all facilities cater for the disabled in the following ways:

- *Access* – doors and doorways have to be wide enough to allow wheelchair access and ramps must be provided.

- *Parking* – disabled bays must be marked and made available.

- *Provision* – lifts must allow access to upper floors, disabled toilets must be provided, and there should be specific activities, clubs or classes that are particularly suited to the disabled.

Study tip

It is important to know how the disabled are catered for to enable them to be active participants. You should also be aware of some examples of how and when they compete.

1.3 Gender

The particular sex of a participant is not something that is within their control, but it is factor that has to be considered for the following reasons.

Physical differences

It is not a sexist view to state that there are differences between males and females because this is a scientifically proven fact.

- Body shape, size and **physique** are generally different in men and women. Women tend to be smaller overall with a flatter, broader pelvis (evolved for childbirth), smaller lungs and heart and a higher percentage of fat (25 per cent for young females compared to 15 per cent for young males). This will also be affected by diet, which has an effect on **metabolic** rate.

- Because women have smaller hearts and lungs, they also have a lower oxygen-carrying capacity than males – there can be a difference of up to 43 per cent!

- Muscle strength and **power** can vary. In tests for **maximal strength** there was a difference of up to 40 to 50 per cent, as women have less total muscle mass.

- Women have less muscle mass than men so they tend to be far more flexible.

- Rates of maturity differ, with girls tending to mature faster than boys. For this reason some competition between younger males and females can be fair, but from the age of 11 upwards males start to overtake in terms of height and strength, so sport tends to becomes single sex after this age.

- The fact that females menstruate and suffer a hormonal imbalance can disadvantage females if they are participating during their period. Males tend to be less effected by chemical substance changes within their bodies.

A *Men have a greater muscle mass than women so would find it easier to be a well-developed body builder*

Objectives

Consider the differences that exist between males and females.

Consider the physical, metabolic and hormonal differences that exist.

Consider the allowances that are made in view of these differences and because of the effects they can have.

∞ links

There are links to physique on pages 18–19, as well as cultural and social factors in Chapter 9 and diet in Chapter 4.

∞ links

These points also relate to training in Chapter 6.

Key terms

Physique: the form, size and development of a person's body.

Metabolic: the whole range of biochemical processes that occur within us.

Power: the combination of speed and strength.

Maximal strength: the greatest amount of weight that can be lifted in one go.

These differences do not always mean that women are disadvantaged, as they are often able to compete on equal terms with men in many situations. There can also be advantages, with less weight and greater flexibility, in sports such as gymnastics. However, they may be seriously disadvantaged when it comes to competing in events dependent on strength and power. These differences are recognised and it is for this reason that competition between males and females is organised in single sexes at the top level. This is also why males and females are judged against the criteria and not against each other for GCSE PE practical purposes!

B *Equestrian events are one of the few events where women compete against men head to head and not in separate competitions*

Perceived differences

- Discrimination has often meant that women are seen as the 'weaker sex' and not allowed the same opportunities as men. They were not allowed to compete in distance races greater than 800 metres in the Olympics until 1960 – the 1,500 metres was added in 1972 and the 10,000 metres in 1988. Many other sports are seen as traditionally male and it is only recently that football has seen a surge in female players to make it the fastest growing sport. Some women may also find that their religion forbids them to take part fully as they have to remain covered as a requirement of their faith and this can restrict their opportunities to participate.

- Historically there have been fewer opportunities for women. It is only comparatively recently that women have been granted equal opportunities to become officials, managers and so on.

Study tip

You should be able to identify some of the physiological differences between men and women and back this up with knowledge about why competition is usually single sex. You may also be asked about sexual discrimination in sport.

1.4 Culture

The particular **culture** in which an individual lives or is brought up is bound to have a significant influence on their life. In particular, it is likely to be a factor that may affect their levels of participation in physical education and sporting activities.

Participation influences

Different cultures and societies can often have varying priorities, and taking part in sport either in or out of school can be one of those priorities for many of the following reasons:

- The cultural traditions and historical background of a society (country or nation) will set the scene for what is considered to be normal and acceptable within that culture. Within the UK there is a mixture of cultures that are all accepted by each other, and there is also a wide range of choice in terms of sporting activities that any individual can take part in. Within the examination specification that you are studying, there are over 100 different activities which you could choose to be assessed on! Some other cultures have a much narrower range of activities available. Sometimes this is due to economic reasons as they simply do not have enough money to provide facilities for a large range of activities.

- Some cultures make specific choices regarding what to provide. The island of Cuba, in the Caribbean, became a communist state in 1959 and it had close links with the communist state of the USSR. The regime that ruled the country decided to concentrate on a limited number of sporting and athletic activities so that they could be successful in those. From 1961 onwards, only five sports were selected to be taught in secondary schools: track and field athletics, basketball, baseball, gymnastics and volleyball. Baseball was selected as the official sport of Cuba.

- Many other Caribbean countries, for example the West Indies, excel at sports that were introduced into the country by the British when they were part of the British Empire. This is one of the main reasons why the sport of cricket is so popular there. India was also part of the British Empire, which is why cricket was also introduced there and remains so popular today.

Religion

Particular cultures are often linked to specific religions and these religions also have traditional values and guidelines that they sometimes insist are followed.

- Many Muslim cultures have specific dress codes that require certain clothing to be worn. An example of this is cricketer Monty Panesar whose religion is Indian Ramghari Sikh, which requires him to wear a turban as he has uncut hair and a full beard. When he trains and plays, Monty wears a black patka (a smaller version of the full Sikh turban).

- Many Muslims **fast** during the religious period of Ramadan and this can affect their performance when training and competing.

Objectives

Consider the ways in which different cultures might encourage greater levels of participation than others.

Consider how religion may be a significant factor in some cultures.

Consider how gender may be a significant factor in some cultures.

Key terms

Culture: the ideas, customs and social behaviour of a particular people or society.

Fast: to eat only certain types of food or to reduce food intake.

Devout: devoted or dedicated to.

Gender: the state of being male or female.

Hijab: a head covering that must be worn in public by some Muslim women.

A 100-metre sprinter Tahmina Kohistani has to wear impractical clothing in order to be allowed to compete in her event

- Some **devout** Christians refuse to train or compete on Sundays as this conflicts with their religious belief. A famous example of this was former Olympic, Commonwealth, European and World record holder, triple jumper Jonathan Edwards. His decision not to compete on Sundays cost him the chance to take part in the 1991 World Championships. He did not change his mind until 1993. Some Jewish faith performers also refuse to compete at certain times.

Gender

The factor of **gender** is often linked closely with religion due to the fact that many religions have strict guidelines that apply specifically to females.

- Sprinter Tahmina Kohistani of Afghanistan had to wear a **hijab** and long clothing to conform with Islamic modesty laws when competing in the London 2012 Olympics. Fellow competitor Wojdan Shaherkani, from Saudi Arabia, had similar problems as she had to wear a form of headscarf when competing in the judo competition – at one point judo's governing body considered refusing to allow her to wear it. She became the first ever Saudi Arabian female to compete in any Olympics.
- Many females who live in cultures that have extreme religious views find they are harassed by men, racially abused, whistled at and heckled when they are training or competing in their own country.
- In many cultures some sports are not even considered suitable for women to compete in. The sports of women's rugby and football have been introduced and developed in the UK comparatively recently, and in some cultures it would not be deemed appropriate for women to take part in them.

B *Due to his religious beliefs, cricketer Monty Panesar wears his patka when he plays*

⊂◯⊃ links

There are links to balanced and specific diets in Chapter 4.

Activities

1. Find out more about the British Empire in terms of the countries that were part of it and the sporting activities that were introduced into their culture by the British.

2. Find other examples where the religious beliefs of a performer have prevented them from training or competing.

3. Find some recent examples where female performers have had to conform with specific religious rules or codes.

⊂◯⊃ links

Gender is also considered on pages 14 and 15.

Study tip

You need to be aware that culture is an important influence when an individual is choosing a sport or activity to participate in. Questions are likely to focus on a factor relating to culture that is likely to decrease levels of popularity or reduce levels of participation.

1.5 Physique

Physique is very closely linked to body type and it is another one of those factors that an individual has very little control over – your basic physique is something you are born with and which develops naturally. You may be able to influence your **body composition** and **musculature** but your height and general body shape are preordained.

Objectives

Consider the link between body type and somatotype.

Consider the three types of extreme somatotype that exist.

Consider the most suitable body type for a role or position in a particular sport.

Body types

Your body type, or **somatotype**, may well mean that you are particularly suited to a specific sport or it can mean that some activities are more difficult, with less chance of success. The following categories of body type give more guidance on this and are all based on a classification of body types first identified by Sheldon. Note that all the descriptions are for extremes of body type and it is likely that people mostly fall somewhere between these categories and not solely within one.

Endomorph

These people tend to be roughly pear-shaped, with wide hips, wide shoulders, a tendency to gain fat, especially on the upper arms and thighs, and have short legs in relation to their **trunks**. An extreme endomorph will find it difficult to carry out weight-bearing aerobic exercises, such as distance running, but in sports such as rugby their bulk could be an advantage in certain playing positions, such as pack members in the scrum.

Mesomorph

These people have a generally wedge-shaped body with broad, wide shoulders, muscled arms and legs, narrow hips and a minimum amount of fat. An extreme mesomorph can excel in strength, agility and speed sports and they are particularly well suited to swimming events. Their body type is unlikely to make any sports unsuitable for them to participate in at a high level.

∞ links

This links to the structure and role of the muscular system on pages 66–69, and could have implications for training on pages 26–27 and Chapter 6.

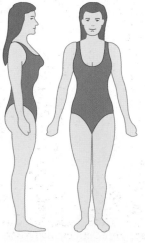

A *Endomorph*   *Mesomorph*   *Ectomorph*

Ectomorph

These people are predominantly long, slender and thin with narrow shoulders and hips, thin arms and legs and very little muscle and body fat. Owing to their slight build they are not suited to power and strength sports but they can succeed at endurance events, such as marathon running and also gymnastics where their light frame is an advantage.

Body type and sport

In most sports it is possible to take part whatever your somatotype is and, while it is possible to grade yourself on a table, no account is made of height in this classification. A tall ectomorph would be very well suited to the high jump and a weightlifter would need to be predominantly a mesomorph, but most games players would not fit into any of these extremes.

B *This basketball player would fit into the category of a tall mesomorph where his height is a distinct advantage*

Activity

Watch the different events in an athletics event or tournament and see where the various somatotypes are very similar and where a particular somatotype is a clear advantage in the event.

Key terms

Body composition: the percentage of body weight that is fat, muscle and bone.

Musculature: the system or arrangement of muscles on a body.

Somatotypes: different body types based on shape, most commonly endomorph, mesomorph and ectomorph.

Trunk: the middle part of your body (midsection).

Study tip

You not only need to know categories of somatotypes but you also need to know specifically how a particular body type could affect the choice of and its suitability for a particular event or activity.

1.6 Environment

The environment is not a single factor – you may have a degree of control over some environmental factors whereas you will not over some others. However, all the factors can have an effect on participation.

■ Weather

This is a factor that you may have no control over, but a professional performer might be able to afford to go to a country where the weather is suitable – cold and snowy for a skier or warm and dry for a tennis player. Weather affects both training and competing separately.

Training

If you are a marathon runner you need to carry out distance runs as part of your training, which you might not be able to do if there is snow or ice. Similarly, a tennis player might only have access to outdoor courts and would not play in rain, snow or cold, icy weather.

Competing

Many activities stop if the weather is poor. This includes being too hot, too cold, too wet, too dry (hard grounds), too foggy, too windy or during thunder storms.

A *Heavy rain, resulting in floods, can cause either training or competition events to be stopped*

■ Pollution

Air pollution can affect both training and competing because it is a serious health risk for anyone taking exercise in such conditions. If pollution levels are high then performing outside will not be possible, so training is restricted to indoors and where there is air conditioning or some form of climate control.

Activity

1   Make a log of how often school PE activities are interrupted or stopped because of the weather. Can you find examples of each of the conditions mentioned?

∞ links

These factors link to training in Chapter 6 and the physical and mental demands of performance in Chapter 2. There are also considerations for health and safety covered on pages 144–145.

Altitude

This is the height of an area above sea level. Training and performing at high altitude can be a real benefit (see pages 86–87 for specific information about this) and living and training at high altitude all the time can be a real advantage for someone if they take part in endurance events.

Humidity

This relates to the amount of water vapour that is in the air. Humidity combined with heat makes conditions very difficult for performers to keep their bodies cool enough and to avoid **dehydration**. In the World Cross Country Championships in 2007, high levels of humidity resulted in 20 per cent of the competitors failing to complete the distance in the four races.

Terrain

The **landscape** you require may be crucial to your sport because, for example, you would need slopes and snow as a skier and sea and surf as a surfer. Climbers need challenges to climb and cyclists might need flat ground for speed trails or hills for mountain biking.

B   *This mountain-bike rider needs steep slopes to be able to train for and take part in events*

Key terms

Dehydration: the rapid loss of water from the body.

Landscape: the aspect of the land characteristic of a particular region.

Activity

2   Try to match each of these terrain-linked environmental factors to actual examples where training and competition has had to stop due to the environment not being suitable or safe.

Study tip

It is important to be aware of all of these factors and acknowledge that performers' ability to overcome problems caused by the environment can vary.

1.7 Risk and challenge

One of the main appeals to many participants of physical activity is that it offers them both a **challenge** and an acceptable level of **risk**. This must always remain in balance to ensure that activities are safe and suitable.

Challenging activities

Some activities are clearly far more challenging than others.

- Outdoor and adventurous activities clearly have many challenges. Anyone taking part in climbing is going to have to cope with a challenging environment in terms of height and difficult climbs. Any water-based sport, such as canoeing or surfing, means that you may take part in possibly difficult water conditions. These types of activity require the environment to be challenging in order to make taking part worthwhile and will often have scales of challenge. Once a certain condition or area has been dealt with, there is then another level to confront.

- Challenge within activities can also be a factor. To tackle a bigger opponent in rugby is a physical challenge, as is to run in excess of 26 miles in a marathon.

Objectives

Consider the aspect of challenge that is present in physical activity.

Consider the need for carrying out risk assessment.

Consider the importance of being aware of risk control.

Key terms

Challenge: a test of your ability or resources in a demanding situation.

Risk: the possibility of suffering harm, loss or danger.

A *This climber is well aware of the level of challenge present*

Activity

Carry out a survey to find out which of the activities offered within your school is considered to be the most challenging, both physically and mentally.

Risk assessment

It is vital that potential hazards or dangers are spotted before any physical activity is undertaken. All aspects of the sporting environment have to be considered in order to be sure that a degree of challenge is still present but that safety is fully considered.

B   *These boxers wear protective gloves and head guards to minimise the risk when taking part in their chosen activity*

Risk control

This means that every effort has to be made by the participants and those in charge to ensure that the activity continues in a safe manner once the correct level of risk assessment has been carried out.

- Participants should always perform properly within the rules and regulations of their activity and avoid foul play and inappropriate behaviour. This could include making sure that their equipment is in good order (sharp studs of football boots could badly injure another player) and that they are not wearing any jewellery.
- Organisers need to ensure that they are fully qualified and knowledgeable to be in charge of a group so they do not mix age or gender groups, they do not have too many people taking part and that the group has warmed up properly.

▊ Safeguards

It is important to always have first-aid equipment available and be aware of where qualified first aiders or telephones are located in case it is necessary to contact the emergency services.

∞ links

Taking on the role of an organiser for part of the practical assessment is considered on pages 116–117 and in Chapter 13.

Study tip

Questions are often asked about why an individual would want to take part in a challenging activity. They are also linked to being aware of the safety measures that must be considered in a particular activity.

1.8 Activity levels and needs

Levels of activity and needs will obviously vary between individuals and have to be considered under the two headings of the specific needs and the effects that will result because of these activity levels.

Activity needs

Activity needs will vary between different activities because they will all place varying demands on the performer, as shown in the following examples:

- **Competitive** activities require performers to be highly committed as they need to train to compete. This might well mean two training sessions in a week, which might be further broken down into fitness training and skill training, followed by a competitive match over the weekend. A cricketer might have to be prepared to give up a full day for any match they are involved in and even a netball player may have to set aside a full day to travel to a game fixture. If a performer is a professional competitor, they will concentrate on their particular activity full time.

- **Recreational** activities are not as demanding, as these types of activity do not require any periods of special training or preparation. The only requirement is to take part in the activity for some length of time and at a convenient time.

A *Most games of cricket demand that at least a day is spent to complete a match*

- Performance levels are a factor, as someone who is performing at the top level of their sport, such as an area, county or international competitor would find that they have to dedicate a lot of time to being an active participant.
- Individual factors, such as age, may also be an influence as a younger person who is at school may have more leisure time to take part in activity than an adult in a full-time job.

B *Bowls is an activity often played by older participants as it does not have high levels of physical demand*

Activity effects

The level at which you perform is also going to have an effect on you.

- High levels of participation are likely to bring with them benefits, which are highlighted in Chapter 5. The health benefits to be gained will be clearly identified, but these benefits can only be maintained if the levels of participation are continued on a regular basis. There are also other benefits, such as the enjoyment of the social aspect of taking part with others and the satisfaction of successful competition.
- Low and infrequent levels of activity clearly have little or no positive effect.

Activity

Find a sportsperson who performs at least at county level and interview them about the demands made on them in competing at that level.

⃝⃝links

This links to many of the individual factors in Chapter 1, especially pages 10–13, as well as to Chapter 3, which deals with leisure and recreation.

Study tip

It is important to be able to compare and contrast the levels and needs linked to the demands of different activities and to be able to back this up with some actual examples.

1.9 Training

This is clearly a factor that the individual has almost total control over and, to some degree, they can decide how much or little they do.

Level of participation

Someone taking part in sport at the highest level will seek to train as often as possible. For some performers this can be on a daily basis and they would have to consider **periodisation**. This is carried out to ensure that they are able to **peak** at the right time, usually to coincide with a major competition or tournament. This takes into account their competitive year, which would consist of the following:

- *The pre-season* – this is the time leading up to when the majority of the competition will take place and is a time of initial preparation, concentrating on fitness and even developing techniques specific to the activity.

- *Peak season* – this is the main competitive period and there would need to be a concentration on skills, ongoing fitness sessions as well as taking part in the actual competition.

A *Wayne Rooney and Rio Ferdinand taking part in a Manchester United pre-season training session*

■ *Post-season (or off-season)* – this is mainly a period of rest and recovery but there is still a need to keep up levels of **general fitness**.

In many activities now there are all-year-round demands on performers – many cricketers play in England during the summer and Australia in the winter so that they never have an off-season.

Available time

This is probably the most crucial factor for most performers as they will only have a totally free choice of available time if they are professional. In order to become a better performer, time is needed to train, but you may only be able to get to a higher level if you train more and this can become a vicious circle. For an amateur performer, fitting in their training can be very difficult. Many swimmers, for example, have to train at their local pools very early in the morning, before the pool is open for public use.

B   *Swimmers often have to train on their own and at odd hours to make use of pools when the public are not using them*

Available funds

The amount of money you have available will also have an effect, as more funding can mean more time, better training facilities and equipment, and even the possibility of hiring a specialist trainer or fitness coach. This is why many sports performers seek sponsorship to enable them to train, either at a higher level or more regularly.

Activity

Carry out a survey of your group, looking at the different levels of training that occur, in terms of time and the costs involved.

Study tip

You are likely to be asked to consider the link between the amount of training an individual is able to undertake in relation to their performance and the factors that effect this and the success that is likely.

1

In this chapter you have learnt:

✔ how an individual's age can affect their levels of participation and which activities might be more suited to particular age groups

✔ the range of disabilities that exist and the ways in which disabled performers are still able to participate

✔ that differences exist between males and females and how these differences can affect participation levels and type

✔ the influence that culture can have on an individual's choice of activities

✔ what is meant by body type and how this can influence the types of activities an individual is most suited to

✔ the effect that the environment can have and how this can affect participation

✔ the risk and challenges that exist in activities and the safe way to deal with them

✔ what different activity levels and needs there are and how these affect participation

✔ how different factors can affect an individual's opportunities to train.

Revision questions

1 Which of the following factors affecting levels of participation do you have total control over?
  a Age
  b Risk and challenge
  c Gender
  d Disability

2 Explain why the majority of sporting events are arranged in particular age groups.

3 Outline two physiological changes that occur with increasing age.

4 What is meant by 'a policy of inclusion'?

5 Explain how an activity could be adapted to allow disabled performers to participate.

6 Describe two physical differences that exist between males and females.

7 In what ways have females suffered from discrimination in terms of their levels of participation in sport?

8 Explain how the culture in which a person grows up might affect the type of activity they decide to participate in.

9 Name the three extremes of body type identified by Sheldon.

10 For one of the identified body types, describe a sport or event they would be particularly suited to and explain why this is so.

11 Why would some individuals choose to take part in an activity involving risk?

12 What is meant by 'periodisation' in relation to training?

13 How can a lack of funds restrict the levels of training possible?

2 Physical and mental demands of performance

Aims

✔ Consider what fatigue and stress are, the reasons why they occur and the effects they can have.

✔ Be aware of the ways in which injury can occur, the types of injury and the precautions that can be taken to avoid injury.

✔ Be aware of common injuries and what action should be taken if an accident, injury or emergency does occur.

✔ Be aware of the components of the respiratory system, the action of breathing and the process of gaseous exchange.

✔ Know what is meant by aerobic respiration and the activities that require it.

✔ Know what is meant by anaerobic respiration, the activities that require it and the recovery process from vigorous exercise.

✔ Be aware of the circulatory system and its component parts, together with the functions they perform and the role and function of the heart.

✔ Be aware of the cardiovascular system and cardiovascular endurance, together with ways to monitor and improve endurance levels.

This chapter focuses on factors affecting your performance. Some factors you will have some level of control over, but some you will not, such as injury – you may not be able to avoid injury at some time but you should be able to take all reasonable precautions to avoid getting one. There is also some basic information regarding first aid and identifying specific conditions and injuries, but it must be stressed that if you are in any doubt you must seek medical help at all times.

This chapter considers three body systems that are most closely linked to the physical demands of performance – it is essential that you are familiar with them and are aware of the ways in which they can be improved, in turn bringing about an improvement in fitness and endurance levels. These are also linked to fatigue and stress as there is a very fine line between putting a strain on your cardiovascular system in order to improve it and overloading it, and consequently suffering from fatigue. You will need to manage this extra demand with this in mind.

2.1 Fatigue and stress

Both fatigue and stress are capable of having a significant impact on performance and it is important that you are aware of the effects they can have. It is also vital that you remember that a different personality type will deal with events in different ways, so emotions have to be dealt with individually too.

Fatigue

Fatigue is a feeling of extreme physical or mental tiredness brought on by extreme exertion and it can result in temporary loss of strength and energy. If you suffer from fatigue, the following is likely to occur:

- Your body or parts of your body may not be able to carry on with what you are doing due to **local muscular fatigue** and it can even result in you having to stop what you are doing completely.
- Concentration levels will decrease and you are more likely to make mistakes of judgement.
- Skill levels decrease as speed and strength decrease.
- If you are not able to have some form of rest, you will be forced to stop.

This can be a dangerous condition and carrying on can result in injury, often brought about by the fact that techniques will not be performed as well. This is one of the reasons why substitutions are allowed in many major sports so that coaches and managers are able to replace players when they see the signs of fatigue becoming apparent.

∞ links

This links closely to the muscular system pages 66–69.

A *This rugby player is being substituted as the effects of fatigue have set in*

Activity

The next time you are taking part in a strenuous physical activity see how many of the effects of fatigue you are able to identify and consider the overall effect this had on your performance.

Stress

Stress is the body's reaction to a change that requires a physical, mental or emotional adjustment or response and this, in turn, can be linked to other factors in any sporting situation. Some people may become more aggressive and others may find that levels of arousal are increased.

- Excitement or suspense can lead to tension. If this is experienced before taking part in an activity it can result in tightness in the muscles, which could then have a physical effect.

- Anxiety can make you feel uneasy and **apprehensive** both before and during performance. If you become over anxious, you are likely to make mistakes. However, most performers consider some level of anxiety to be necessary to help them to focus and prepare.

- Nervousness can add to your tension levels, making you feel more tense and even agitated to the point where it can have a physical effect such as shaking or feeling sick.

- **Motivation** will almost certainly decrease.

Almost everyone who has ever taken part in physical activity has experienced stress and it is far more common in individual activities where the focus is on one person. However, even in team games it can occur – most batters walking out to bat will have experienced it!

Participants who become bored easily or who find aspects of either practicing or performing tedious are likely to achieve less as performers.

B *Walking out to bat in a match can be very stressful with feelings of tension and anxiety building up*

Key terms

Local muscular fatigue: when a muscle, or group of muscles, is unable to carry on contracting and movement stops.

Apprehensive: fearful about the future.

Motivation: your drive to succeed and desire and energy to achieve something.

∞ links

This links closely to skill-related factors of fitness on pages 72–73 where motivation is considered in more detail.

Study tip

Questions on this topic are likely to include being able to identify clearly what fatigue and stress are and what affect they are likely to have on performance.

2.2 Injury

The chances of getting an injury through taking part in physical activity are quite high and most performers experience one at some time. The essential point to bear in mind is that injury prevention should be paramount and that all possible precautions should be taken in order to avoid it and minimise the risk.

Techniques and safe practice

It is important that correct techniques are used at all times and there are countless examples where using a poor technique has resulted in an injury to both performers and opponents. These injuries can be considered to be in the categories of internally and externally caused injuries.

Internally caused injuries

These are injuries where a performer is solely responsible.

- *Overuse injuries* – these can be caused by either training or performing too much and can include **stress fractures** and muscle and tendon injuries. Tennis players can suffer from **tennis elbow** and many footballers suffer from cartilage damage.

- *Sudden injuries* – when you are taking part in physical activity there is also a strain put on the body owing to lots of stretching, twisting and turning, often resulting in problems, such as hamstring pulls.

Externally caused injuries

These can be caused by factors other than the performer themselves, such as by the equipment, an opponent or even the playing conditions.

- *Foul play or incorrect actions (including poor or incorrect technique)* – this involves other players, usually opponents, and these types of injuries can often be quite serious, which is why there are rules to prevent them happening.

- *Impact injuries* – many activities permit physical contact within the rules of the game (hockey, rugby and football, for example) so contact is inevitable, but it also occurs in many other activities such as in netball and basketball. There can also be impact with equipment, such as goal posts, football boots, hockey sticks or vaulting boxes, and impact with the playing surface itself, such as an outdoor court area, a sports hall floor or artificial turf.

Objectives

Consider the ways in which injuries might be caused and the type of injury that results.

Consider the precautions that can be taken to prevent injuries occurring.

Key terms

Stress fracture: a break in the bone caused by repeated application of a heavy load or constant pounding on a surface, such as by running.

Tennis elbow: a painful injury or inflammation of the tendon attached to the elbow joint.

A *A distance runner puts a considerable strain on their bones owing to constant pounding during training runs, often resulting in stress fractures*

- *Equipment/clothing* – this could be equipment that is damaged (such as splinters from damaged hockey sticks), faulty (such as non-fixed portable goals) or badly fitting, such as trainers that are too tight causing blisters, or inappropriate clothing, such as baggy clothing in trampolining.

- *Accidents* – whatever precautions are in place, there will always be some accidents.

∞ links

This section links closely to pages 144–147 where health and safety, and sport and equipment rules are dealt with in greater detail.

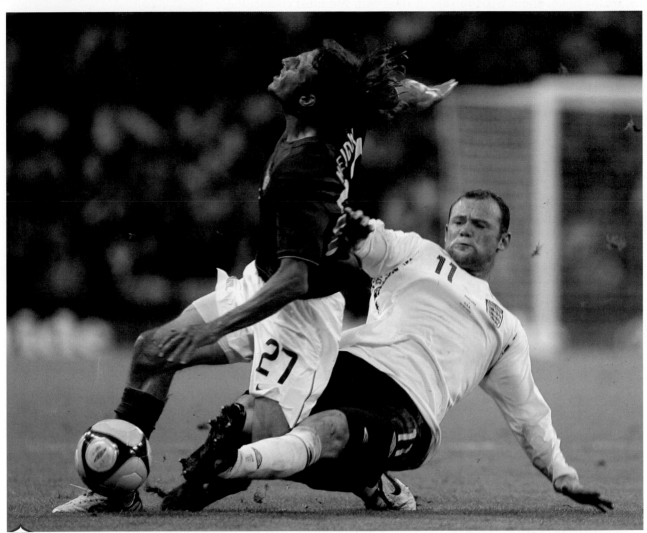

B   *Wayne Rooney stretching to tackle Frankie Hejduk of the USA. Impacts such as this occur regularly in any game of football*

Activity

Carry out a survey regarding all of the injuries that members of your group have experienced within the last year and categorise them as internally or externally caused injuries. Which is the longer list?

▮ Precautions

The following is a basic precautionary guide:

- A risk assessment should be carried out and the findings followed.
- Warm-ups should always be carried out before starting.
- All rules or codes of conduct should be clear, followed and enforced.

Study tip

The important aspect of this section is that injuries should be prevented so you should know the most common causes and the steps that should be taken to prevent them. You may also be asked to use examples in your answers.

2.3 First aid and emergency arrangements

Accidents and injuries do occur so it is very important to know what to do if they happen. The most important thing to bear in mind is that you will not become an expert after reading this section and that if you are in any doubt about what you are dealing with you **must** contact the emergency services.

Common injuries

- *Head injuries* – you must make sure that the injured person is able to breathe and put them in the coma position, making sure that their mouth and nose are clear. Concussion can occur and this can be apparent from a loss of consciousness, very relaxed limbs, weak and irregular pulse, slow and shallow breathing, **dilated** pupils and even bleeding from the ears. Concussion is definitely a condition that must be dealt with by experts.

- *Fractures* – these are broken bones and usually occur on the upper or lower limbs. Often a snapping sound can be heard when it happens but other signs include pain in the area, the shape and outline of the limb is abnormal or it is in an unnatural position, there is considerable swelling and you might actually see the bone sticking out.

- *Hypothermia* – this is a rapid cooling of the body when the temperature drops very quickly. If the person is wearing wet clothing, remove this immediately and cover them with warm dry clothing or blankets.

Objectives

Be aware of the action to be taken if an accident or emergency occurs.

Have a knowledge of the common injuries associated with different activities.

Be able to identify particular injuries and be aware of the actions that might be taken.

Key terms

Dilated: enlarged, expanded or widened.

Sprains: the overstretching or tearing of ligaments at a joint.

Strains: the overstretching of a muscle, rather than a joint.

A *This person has been placed in the recovery position to ensure that all of their airways are clear*

B   *Jermain Defoe of Tottenham is suffering from cramp. Joleon Lescott of Manchester City is straightening his limb to help him relieve it.*

- *Joint and muscle injuries* – these include **sprains**, **strains**, pulled muscles, cramp and dislocations. When these occur you should apply the RICE principle, which is:

  REST – stop straight away and rest the injury.

  ICE – try to apply some ice as it reduces swelling and relieves some of the pain. Do not apply it directly but use an ice pack.

  COMPRESSION – put on a bandage or some tape to give support and pressure to the injured area. Do not put this on too tightly or it can cause further problems by restricting the blood flow.

  ELEVATION – try to raise the injured body part to decrease the circulation to the area and drain away any other fluids.

  This principle applies to any soft tissue injury, so it can be used for any ligament or muscle injury and also helps when bruising has occurred.

Cuts

These can vary in size and seriousness, but all cuts should be dealt with. If possible, clean and dress the cut with a plaster for a small cut and a bandage for a more serious one.

links

These pages link closely to injury on pages 32–33 as well as health and safety on pages 144–145 and sport and equipment rules on pages 146–147. They also link specifically to Chapter 6 for double-award candidates.

Study tip

Only those people taking the Double Award are likely to be examined, but it is important for everyone to know the difference between a sprain and a strain and to know what is meant by **RICE**.

Activity

Carry out a survey to see how many of the identified injuries have been sustained by different members of your group during physical activity. Make a note of the most frequent and common ones.

2.4 The respiratory system: aerobic

The diagram below shows the respiratory system where the air is taken in through the mouth and travels to the lungs, into the bronchioles and into the lungs where **gaseous exchange** occurs in the **alveoli**.

Aerobic respiration

Aerobic respiration is summarised as **respiration that occurs in the presence of oxygen** and is:

glucose + oxygen → energy + carbon dioxide + water

This type of respiration is used when the body continues an activity for a long period of time and the energy to do so is produced using oxygen. In order for the aerobic system to work efficiently, there has to be a constant supply of oxygen to the body. This is important for any activity that is going to be performed for a sustained period of time.

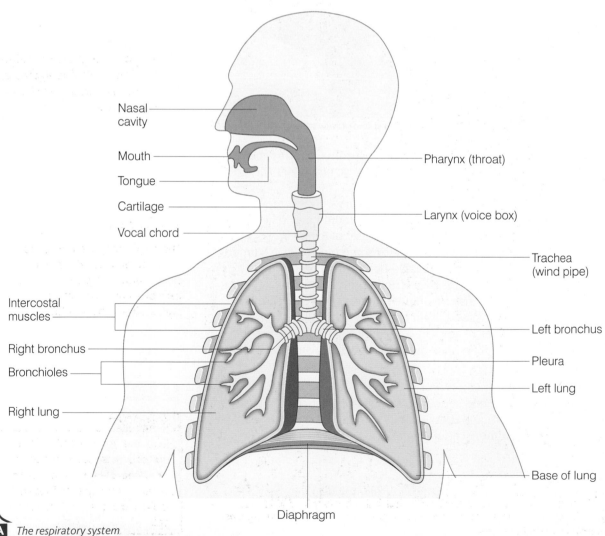

Nasal cavity

Mouth

Tongue

Cartilage

Vocal chord

Pharynx (throat)

Larynx (voice box)

Trachea (wind pipe)

Intercostal muscles

Right bronchus

Bronchioles

Right lung

Left bronchus

Pleura

Left lung

Base of lung

Diaphragm

A The respiratory system

The action of breathing

When we breathe in, the chest cavity changes shape and size – the diaphragm changes from a dome shape as it flattens and moves downwards. As this is happening, the **intercostal muscles** raise the ribs up and push out the **sternum**, which makes the cavity larger. This serves to reduce the pressure inside the chest cavity and causes air to be sucked into the lungs. The air we are actually breathing in is high in oxygen and nitrogen but low in carbon dioxide.

When we breathe out, the reverse process occurs but the air breathed out is high in nitrogen and carbon dioxide as the full process of gaseous exchange has taken place.

Breathing rate

Breathing rate increases greatly when we exercise. It can increase up to three times the rate when we are at rest.

B   *This runner has completed some vigorous aerobic exercise and is trying to get her breathing rate back to normal*

Key terms

Gaseous exchange: the process where oxygen is taken in from the air and exchanged for carbon dioxide.

Alveoli: small air sacs in the lungs where gaseous exchange takes place.

Intercostal muscles: abdominal muscles inbetween the ribs that assist in the process of breathing.

Sternum: the chest or breastbone.

Activity

Check your own breathing rate at rest and then exercise vigorously for a few minutes and see how high it has risen.

links

The respiratory system has to be considered together with the circulatory systems and the cardiovascular system on pages 40–41 and 42–43.

Study tip

Make sure you understand the process of gaseous exchange and that aerobic respiration is **with** oxygen. Knowing activities that require aerobic respiration is also vital.

2.5 The respiratory system: anaerobic

Anaerobic respiration

While the aerobic system is respiration in the presence of oxygen, **anaerobic respiration occurs in the absence of oxygen** and is summarised as:

$$\text{glucose} \rightarrow \text{energy} \rightarrow \text{lactic acid}$$

This type of respiration occurs when the body works without sufficient oxygen being supplied to the muscles. As oxygen is not being used to generate the energy, it can only be used for short bursts.

Objectives

Consider what is meant by anaerobic respiration and the types of exercise that require it.

Consider what takes place during the recovery period.

Consider the function and role of the blood in this process.

Activity

When you take part in any activity, record how much anaerobic exercise you carry out compared to aerobic exercise. If you are not a performer, carry this out as an observer.

∞ links

This links closely with pages 36–37 and the diagram of the respiratory system. There are also close links to the circulatory system on pages 40–41 and the cardiovascular system on pages 42–43.

A Usain Bolt wins the Olympic 100m final in record time at Beijing 2008. These sprinters are performing anaerobically as they intend to exercise for less than ten seconds.

Oxygen debt

This is what happens as a result of the muscles respiring anaerobically during vigorous exercise because as our bodies run out of sufficient supplies of oxygen we call on **glycogen** stores in the body as an alternative energy supply. We can only respire anaerobically for a maximum of approximately 60 seconds. In this time, we are effectively 'borrowing' oxygen, which is then 'owed' to the body. This is known as our oxygen debt. This will cause a build up of **lactic acid** in the working muscles, which will make the muscles hurt. One of the main reasons for completing a warm-down after exercise is to enable the lactic acid to disperse and avoid this discomfort.

B *Usain Bolt is combining his warm-down with his lap of honour, allowing the lactic acid to disperse to avoid later discomfort*

The recovery period

Straight after any vigorous exercise we have to take in extra oxygen (feeling short of breath after this exercise is completely normal and experienced by everyone), which helps to convert the possibly painful presence of lactic acid into simple waste products that have to be removed from the body.

- *Expiration of breath* – removes the carbon dioxide and other waste products from our lungs.

- *Perspiration* – is a form of temperature control and also removes excess water such as sweat at the same time that it is letting heat escape through evaporation from the skin. Although this heat is not really a waste product, it must be released to prevent our bodies from overheating.

- *Excretion though urine and faeces* – removes excess water and the other waste products from the lactic acid.

Role of the blood

As well as controlling body temperature, one of the most basic roles of the blood is as a transporter and it is through this function that the oxygen, glucose and waste products are all transported around the body. This is dealt with in greater detail on pages 40–41 (The circulatory system).

This is dealt with in greater detail on pages 40–41 (The circulatory system).

Key terms

Glycogen: the main form of carbohydrate storage, which is converted into glucose as needed by the body to satisfy its energy needs.

Lactic acid: a mild poison and waste product of anaerobic respiration.

Study tip

It is crucial that you are able to identify the difference between aerobic and anaerobic exercise and respiration. You should be able to give good examples of activities for both.

2.6 The circulatory system

The circulatory system carries and transports the blood as the body's fuel supply around the body, as the diagram below illustrates.

Functions of the circulatory system

The basic function is to transport by carrying blood. Working together with the respiratory system, this achieves the following:

- The blood carries the oxygen, water and nutrients throughout the body and transports and removes the waste.
- Protection is provided when antibodies that fight infection are carried in the blood. Blood can clot to seal cuts and wounds.

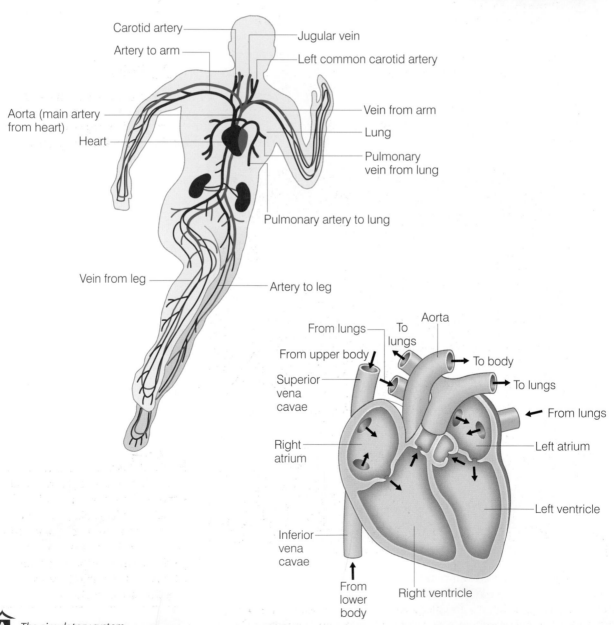

A The circulatory system

- Body temperature is regulated as the blood absorbs body heat and carries it to the lungs and skin where it is released.

The heart

The heart is basically a very efficient pump. Like any other muscle it contracts and relaxes – every instance in which it does this is called a heartbeat, with an average of about 72 heartbeats per minute for an adult at rest. This **heart rate** will increase with exercise as the heart is called upon to supply more oxygen to the working muscles. It has to increase quite considerably to be able to cope with strenuous exercise.

Blood vessels

Blood vessels allow the blood to flow. There are three different types:

- *Arteries* – these have thick walls and carry the oxygenated blood at high pressure away from the heart through the aorta. They do not have any valves and have quite elastic walls. Your **pulse** can be located in arteries.
- *Veins* – these carry the deoxygenated blood back to the heart. They have thinner walls than arteries, which are less elastic. They also have valves to make sure that the blood does not flow backwards.
- *Capillaries* – these are microscopic vessels that link the arteries to the veins and are very thin to allow oxygen and carbon dioxide to pass through their walls.

⃝⃝links

These pages must be considered with pages 36–39 as these systems do not work in isolation.

Key terms

Heart rate: the number of times your heart beats in one minute, which is one contraction and relaxation of the heart.

Pulse: a recording of the rate per minute at which the heart beats.

⃝⃝links

The increase in heart rate and reasons for this are dealt with in more detail on pages 42–43, looking at the cardiovascular system.

B   *The easiest place to check your pulse is on your wrist, as shown here*

Study tip

You will not need to know exact details about the heart or be required to label diagrams, but you must be aware of the function of the circulatory system, that it deals with transport and how it links to the respiratory and cardiovascular systems.

Activity

Practise locating, taking and recording your pulse – this will be vital for later tasks! Try to find out about three other possible pulse points.

The cardiovascular system

This is the name given to the system, consisting of the heart and blood vessels, that circulates blood and transports oxygen around the body. This is the body system that is referred to when considering the respiratory and circulatory systems working together in unison.

Cardiovascular endurance

This is the ability of the heart and lungs to keep supplying oxygen in the bloodstream to the body in order to provide the energy to sustain physical movement. This means that when someone takes part in an activity that requires them to keep moving for long periods of time, they need to ensure that they take this aspect into account and try to improve it.

When you take part in sustained activity, you will notice the following effects:

- An increase in your breathing rate
- An increase in your heart rate (pulse)
- An increase in your **blood pressure**.

This is because your working muscles require additional oxygen, providing the energy supply, because there has been a greater demand put upon them.

Improving cardiovascular endurance

This is an essential requirement for all participants in physical activity so it should be a target for everyone to either improve their levels of endurance or maintain them at a high standard.

The only way to achieve this is to make your heart and lungs work harder in order to get them to adapt to the extra demand. To achieve this you have to keep your heart rate at a high level for some time. The graph shows the levels your pulse rate should be raised to relative to your age using the calculation:

$$\text{MHR} = 220 - \text{your age}$$

Objectives

Be aware what the cardiovascular system consists of.

Understand what is meant by cardiovascular endurance.

Consider the ways in which levels of cardiovascular endurance can be measured and improved.

links

These pages need to be considered in conjunction with pages 36–41.

links

For further details of cardiovascular endurance specifically linked to training see pages 82–83. For details on locating and testing pulse rate see pages 40–41.

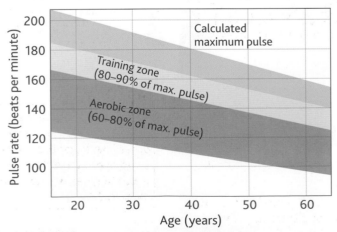

A A pulse rate graph

You should aim to work within the aerobic zone, where you are breathing aerobically and the **training zone** for at least 15 minutes to be able to gain the full benefits of the exercise, so it is important to build up your efforts gradually and make sure you do not try to do too much too quickly.

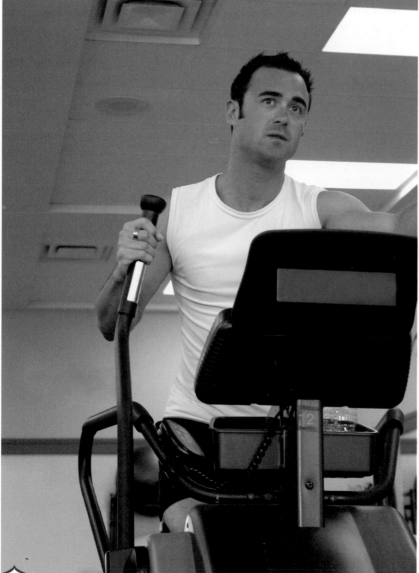

B   *This apparatus has built-in heart-rate monitors in the hand grips, which can help you monitor your heart rate while exercising*

Testing cardiovascular endurance

Check your levels of cardiovascular endurance in the following ways:

- *Resting pulse rate* – this is a general indicator, as the lower this is the better your endurance level is.
- *Pulse recovery rate* – the quicker this returns to the normal, resting rate, the higher your endurance levels are.

This means that you can monitor your pulse over a period of time to try to speed up your recovery rate and, in the longer term, get your resting pulse rate down to a lower level.

Key terms

Blood pressure: the force of the circulating blood on the walls of the arteries.

MHR: maximum heart rate (220 minus age).

Training zone: the range of the heart rate within which a specific training effect will take place.

Activities

1   Find out the resting pulse rates for your entire group and work out the average. Is there a difference between males and females?

2   You should be aware of your levels of cardiovascular endurance, so test your levels by finding out your pulse recovery rate and try to set up some sort of training programme whereby you can monitor and improve it.

Study tip

Questions on this topic are likely to relate to why levels of cardiovascular endurance are important and the ways in which they can be improved and measured.

In this chapter you have learnt:

- ✔ what stress and fatigue are, how they can occur and the effects they can have

- ✔ the types of injury that are common, how they are caused and the precautions you can take to avoid suffering from them

- ✔ basic first aid and emergency arrangements

- ✔ the components that make up the respiratory system

- ✔ the action of breathing and gaseous exchange and how this is linked to aerobic respiration

- ✔ what is meant by anaerobic respiration (the difference between this and aerobic respiration), activities that require it and what occurs during the recovery period immediately after vigorous exercise

- ✔ the circulatory system and the components that make it up

- ✔ the role and function of the heart in the transport of blood

- ✔ the role of the cardiovascular system and its link with the respiratory and circulatory systems

- ✔ how it is possible to monitor and improve levels of cardiovascular endurance.

Revision questions

1. Which of the following would not be classed as an externally caused injury?
   a. Compound fracture
   b. Greenstick fracture
   c. Open fracture
   d. Stress fracture

2. Describe exactly what is meant by fatigue.

3. What effects is fatigue going to have on a performer?

4. Explain what is meant by an overuse injury.

5. Explain why using the correct technique is vital when preventing injuries.

6. What is meant by the RICE principle?

7. Give a simple definition of what aerobic respiration is.

8. Where does gaseous exchange take place?

9. What happens to the breathing rate when you exercise?

10. Give a simple definition of anaerobic respiration.

11. What is oxygen debt?

12. What is the cardiovascular system?

13. How can you measure cardiovascular endurance?

14. How could you improve cardiovascular endurance?

3 Leisure and recreation

■ Aims

✔ Consider what is actually meant by leisure time.

✔ Consider the choices individuals have about how they make use of their leisure time.

✔ Consider the benefits to be gained by becoming involved in leisure activities.

✔ Consider what recreation and recreation time are.

✔ Look at the different recreation types and options available.

✔ Consider the link between recreation and leisure and the benefits to be gained by being active for life.

This chapter focuses on the benefits to be gained by taking part in leisure and recreation as a way of ensuring that a balanced healthy lifestyle can be established and maintained. One of the main reasons for focusing on this is because this can be an alternative to competitive sport and a possible option leading to a lifetime of sports participation.

Leisure time and recreational opportunities are both growing areas and every individual has freedom of choice regarding how they spend their free time and what they do with it.

Knowing about leisure and recreation options that are available should help an individual to make an educated choice in selecting activities that will bring the maximum amount of benefit in terms of achieving an active, healthy lifestyle and achieving a lifetime of involvement in active sport.

3.1 Leisure

Leisure time is quite simply the time when you can choose what you do. You have to establish some sort of balance in your life as there is a certain amount of time when you have to sleep, eat and maintain good hygiene and there will also be a working period involving a job or school. The time you have left over from this is your leisure time and there are a great number of opportunities and provisions made for this time, both for active leisure and passive leisure.

■ Active leisure

This includes taking part in activities that involve exertion of physical or mental energy and can often include **low-impact** physical activities such as yoga or walking, which expend little energy and have little contact or competition. There are also some high-impact activities such as aerobics or kick-boxing.

Objectives

Consider what is meant by leisure time.

Consider the choices individuals have about how they make use of their leisure time.

Consider the benefits to be gained by becoming involved in active leisure.

A *This yoga class is an excellent example of people choosing to take part in an active leisure pursuit*

■ Passive leisure

This includes activities such as those in which a person does not exert any significant physical or mental energy and this might include going to the cinema, watching television or playing video games. This aspect of leisure time is the one that causes the most concern among many experts as it is thought that many activities do not provide the benefits offered by active leisure activities, although for many people this is when they claim that they are relaxing the most.

Activity

Carry out a survey among your group to find out what the most popular passive leisure activity is.

∞ links

This links closely to recreation on pages 48–49 and also social aspects on pages 110–111.

B   *Playing video games is a common leisure activity*

History of leisure

The word 'leisure' derives from the Latin *licere* meaning 'to be permitted' or 'to be free' and up until Victorian times it was not really a concept that was considered, as many workers could work up to 18-hour shifts and had very little spare time. Chapter 8 deals with the reasons for increased leisure time in more detail (pages 102–103), but the fact that people do now have more leisure time at their disposal means that there is quite a lot of competition within the leisure industry to come up with popular provision.

Leisure provision

Local authorities have a legal responsibility to provide leisure services, which include libraries, swimming pools, playing fields and sports centres. There are an increasing number of **private enterprises** that run a variety of sports-related facilities, but these only operate if a profit can be made and if there is a sufficient demand. This is why location can influence your choices, as **rural areas** generally have less provision than **urban areas**.

Key terms

Low-impact: not strenuous with little or no pressure on the joints.

Private enterprise: a privately owned business not regulated in the same way as a state-owned organisation.

Rural areas: areas outside cities and towns.

Urban areas: geographical areas consisting of towns or cities.

Study tip

You should be aware of what leisure time actually is, the reasons why it has increased and the types of provision that are popular for people today.

3.2 Recreation

Recreation can mean just relaxing and enjoying yourself, but it is increasingly being used to mean doing something that is active and healthy.

Physical recreation

As its name suggests, this is where you would opt to participate for **intrinsic reward** rather than **extrinsic reward**, so you would be aware of the health benefits you would be getting as an individual, for pleasure and for a purposeful use of time.

Activity

1   Find out what the most popular physical recreation activity is within your group.

There are a great many of these activities to choose from and they differ between individuals for some of the following reasons:

- *Age* – some recreational activities might suit more elderly people, such as bowls, while younger people might prefer to try something more active or that reflects a current **trend** such as skateboarding.
- *Location* – you might be very interested in taking up surfing as a recreational activity but if you do not live near a surf beach it would be difficult, as would snowboarding if you don't have any snow.
- *Provision and cost* – there might not be a full range of activities available in your area and even if there were, there might be a cost involved that could prevent you from participating regularly.

However, there are many physical recreation activities, walking being the most common one, which are not restricted by any of the factors identified above.

Objectives

Consider what recreation and recreation time are.

Look at the different recreation types and options available.

Consider the link between recreation and leisure and the benefits to be gained by being active for life.

Key terms

Intrinsic reward: something that gives a person or individual an internal satisfaction derived from doing something well.

Extrinsic reward: something that is done for a particular reward that is visible to others.

Trend: the latest and most popular attraction or activity.

⟳links

These pages link closely with leisure on pages 46–47, with social aspects on pages 110–111 and with age on pages 10–11.

A   *Playing bowls is a popular recreation activity with older people*

Activity

2   Carry out a survey of all the recreation facilities that are available in your local area to see how many different activities are on offer.

Outdoor recreation

Many of these activities are also associated with some degree of challenge, including activities such as climbing, fell walking or caving, which involve you in coping with the natural environment that you encounter. Some water-based activities, such as sailing, windsurfing and canoeing, would also come into this category, as you would have to cope with the natural water environment.

Lifelong sports

To gain the maximum benefit from the use of your leisure time through an active recreation pursuit, it is best if you are able to involve yourself in an activity that can be carried on throughout life. Many sports organisations encourage this by making arrangements for different age groups. Swimming is a good example – many competitions, sessions and clubs are targeted at different age groups to encourage maximum participation.

It is accepted that people are not going to be fully active in all the recreation time they have available, but it is to be hoped that if people know how good remaining active is, in terms of all the health benefits, this will be a major feature of their leisure time.

> **Study tip**
>
> It is important to be able to identify what is meant by recreation, but questions are likely to focus on how the best use can be made of available time to bring about the maximum health benefits.

B *Swimming is an activity that can be carried on throughout life and enjoyed by all ages*

 kerboodle

In this chapter you have learnt:

✔ what is meant by leisure time

✔ the choices that individuals have about the use they can make of leisure time

✔ the benefits that can be gained through becoming involved in leisure activities

✔ what is meant by leisure time and recreation

✔ the different types of recreation and the options available

✔ the link between recreation and leisure and the benefits that can be gained through being active for life.

Revision questions

1 Which of the following would not be considered to be an active leisure activity?
   a Visiting the library
   b Attending a yoga class
   c Rambling
   d Attending an aerobics class

2 What is leisure time?

3 What is meant by a low-impact activity?

4 Describe three different passive leisure activities.

5 What problems might someone who lives in a rural area experience compared to someone living in an urban area when it comes to accessing leisure provisions?

6 What is meant by recreation?

7 What is meant by intrinsic reward?

8 What is meant by extrinsic reward?

9 What sort of physical recreation activity is an elderly person more likely to get involved in?

10 What is meant by a trend? Describe a popular current recreation trend.

11 Describe the leisure and recreation facilities that are likely to be available in a typical community.

12 Describe two different challenging outdoor recreation activities.

13 What are the benefits that are likely to come about through following a lifelong sporting interest?

4 Diet

Aims

✔ Be aware of what constitutes a balanced diet and food types in terms of the nutrients required.

✔ Be aware of the proportions of food that should be consumed to ensure a balanced diet.

✔ Consider some of the problems that can occur through an incorrect diet.

✔ Consider how diet is linked to levels of activity and the correct time to eat food in relation to performing.

✔ Be aware of special diets that particular performers might consider using.

This chapter focuses on dietary needs with regard to maintaining a balanced diet as a contributory factor to maintaining a healthy active lifestyle. It also looks at the particular needs that different activities and categories of performers might have.

Having a correct and appropriate diet is a very high profile issue owing to concerns over child obesity rates and the number of health problems now associated with poor eating habits. Responsibilities have been placed upon schools, in particular, to highlight the need for healthy eating and maintaining a balanced diet throughout life. The need for a correct and healthy diet is seen as one of the major problems facing our society, with a need for people to be more aware and better educated about the foods they should be eating as well as the quantities they should consume.

4.1 Maintaining a balanced diet

■ Nutritional needs

Everyone needs food in order to survive. The **nutrients** in food are:

Carbohydrates

These are separated into simple or complex carbohydrates. Simple carbohydrates, or sugars, include glucose and sugar. Complex carbohydrates, or starches, include pasta, bread and rice. Carbohydrates are one of the main sources of energy and are essential for active people.

Fats

There are three types and they are commonly found in cheese, cream, meat, cooking oils, margarine and butter. Fats are a major source of energy for the body.

Proteins

These are commonly known as 'building blocks' because they are very important in the growth of new tissue. The two main sources of protein are animal products and plant foods, such as beans, lentils, nuts and seeds.

Vitamins

Essential to enable you to maintain good health, vitamins are only required in small quantities and are usually contained in a normal diet.

Objectives

Be aware of what constitutes a balanced diet in terms of the nutrients required.

Be aware of the different food types and the nutrients they contain.

Consider what proportions of food should be consumed to ensure a balanced diet.

Consider the problems that could be caused by an imbalance or deficiency in diet.

Fruit and vegetables

Bread, rice, potatoes, pasta and other starchy foods

Meat, fish, eggs, beans and other non-dairy sources of protein

Foods and drinks high in fat and/or sugar

Milk and dairy foods

FOOD STANDARDS AGENCY

food.gov.uk

A *These are the nutrients that make up a balanced diet. The portions represent a balanced intake.*

Minerals

Also only required in small amounts, minerals are mainly found in vegetables and meats.

Water/fluids

These are absolutely essential because failure to replace lost water can result in **dehydration**. More problems can be caused by lack of water than by lack of food!

Fibre/roughage

This is important as an aid to the digestive system and is contained in cereals, wholegrain bread and oats.

links

These pages link specifically to pages 54–55 and also to a healthy active lifestyle on pages 60–61. Details regarding healthy eating can be found at **www.food.gov.uk**

Dietary considerations

No single food is able to provide all the nutrients the body needs so it is important to eat a variety of foods. There are five main food groups:

- bread, rice, potatoes, pasta and other starchy foods
- fruit and vegetables
- milk and dairy foods
- meat, fish, eggs, beans and other non-dairy sources of protein
- food and drinks high in fat and/or sugar.

The proportions for this are shown in the diagram opposite and you should try to choose different foods from the first four groups every day. The foods in the fifth group are not essential to a healthy diet.

Failing to maintain this balance could result in the following dietary imbalance or deficiencies:

- *Malnutrition* – this is a physical weakness resulting from insufficient food or an unbalanced diet.
- *Obesity* – this is a condition of being extremely fat or overweight, which frequently results in health problems.
- *Anorexia* – this is an eating disorder primarily occurring in girls and women, related to a fear of gaining weight, self-starvation and a distorted **body image**.

B   *This person would be described as being clinically obese, which can be a serious medical condition*

4.2 Specific diets

The starting point for any diet must primarily be that it is balanced. However, there may be particular occasions when a diet may need to be adjusted or even adapted for particular performers and particular activities.

■ Levels of participation

Eating food is necessary to provide the body with energy. Eating the right food will ensure that you have enough energy and that you are also able to maintain the correct body weight for your particular needs.

Energy is needed by the body even when it is at rest, but as soon as you become more active your **basal metabolic rate** is affected and you will need to balance the requirements your body has taken in with the amounts that are being used up. The number of **calories** needs to balance because if you have a higher intake than output you will tend to put on weight and if you are very active you will need to make sure that you are providing for your body adequately.

Objectives

Consider how diet is linked to the levels of activity of individuals.

Consider the correct and appropriate times for food to be eaten.

Consider special diets that particular types of performers might require or use.

Key terms

Basal metabolic rate: the minimum rate of energy required to keep all of the life processes of the body maintained when it is at rest.

Calorie: a unit that measures heat or energy production in the body.

Glycogen: the form of carbohydrate storage, which is converted into glucose as needed by the body to satisfy its energy needs.

A *Tennis players will often eat a banana as an energy source between games at changeover*

∞ links

These pages need to be considered with pages 52–53 on maintaining a balanced diet and also with Chapter 1, particularly pages 10–11.

When to eat is also a factor you need to consider carefully. The basic guidelines for this are:

- *Before activity* – do not eat too close to performing. Try to wait about two hours after eating.
- *During activity* – generally you should not eat during activity but something light and in small quantities, such as a banana, would be fine.
- *After activity* – you should try to leave the same two-hour gap as you did before activity.

Liquids may need to be taken before, during and after the activity to avoid dehydration, but do not take in too much liquid immediately after finishing as this can result in discomfort.

Carbohydrate loading

This is a particular dietary plan that endurance athletes, mainly marathon runners, use involving eating plenty of starch-rich foods, such as pasta, in the week before an important competition or event. The starch increases the amount of **glycogen** in the muscles, which can help to delay tiredness and can improve performance in the end stages of a competition because it is a slow-release form of energy.

B   *These marathon runners are taking part in a 'pasta party' arranged by the marathon race organisers*

High-protein diets

These diets are often used by bodybuilders as a means of building muscle and losing fat. However, it must be remembered that extra protein in itself does not add muscle and high protein foods can be difficult to digest so they should not be eaten just before training or competing.

In this chapter you have learnt:

✔ what constitutes a balanced diet and the nutrients required within it

✔ the different food types and the nutrients that these contain

✔ the proportions of food that should be eaten to make sure you have a balanced diet

✔ some of the problems that can occur through not sticking to a balanced diet

✔ the link that diet has to levels of activity and the correct times when food should be eaten in relation to taking part in physical activity

✔ special diets that are available and that might be used by specific sports performers.

Revision questions

1 Which of the following food groups is not essential for a healthy diet?

  a Fruit and vegetables

  b Food and drinks high in fat and/or sugar

  c Bread, rice, potatoes, pasta and other starchy foods

  d Meat, fish, eggs, beans and other non-dairy sources of protein

2 What are nutrients?

3 Name the two types of carbohydrate and give an example of each one.

4 What is the main benefit of fat as a food source?

5 What are proteins also commonly known as?

6 What is the main source of essential vitamins?

7 In which types of food are minerals mainly found?

8 Why is it essential to maintain levels of fluids/water?

9 What is obesity and how is it caused?

10 What is meant by basal metabolic rate?

11 What is a calorie?

12 What is the time period during which you should not eat both before and after exercise?

13 What is meant by carbohydrate loading and which types of performers would be likely to make use of it?

14 Who might decide to use a high-protein diet? What possible problems could be caused by following this type of diet?

5 Health, fitness and a healthy active lifestyle

Aims

✔ Define what good health is and consider what the components that combine to achieve it are.

✔ Consider the differences between health and fitness and be aware of good exercise habits and benefits to be gained from them.

✔ Know the structure of the skeletal system and the functions that the system performs, including movement via joints.

✔ Know the roles that the skeletal system performs.

✔ Know the structure of the muscular system and the different types of muscle that exist.

✔ Understand that the link between the muscular system and the skeletal system allows movement and know the major muscles involved.

✔ Know the various components of fitness that can be identified and how these can be affected by training.

✔ Understand what the various skill-related factors of fitness are and how they can affect performance.

✔ Know what skills are and how they can be acquired and developed.

This chapter focuses on some of the factors that contribute to ensuring that you are able to lead a healthy, active lifestyle. All the factors in this book will have some contribution to make, but this chapter focuses more specifically on some of the major ones.

There are many daily demands made on the body and a level of fitness is required so that these can be dealt with without undue stress and in comfort. All the factors identified in this chapter can help to keep this level sufficiently high, as well as improve it.

5.1 General health

Good health is something that most people take for granted – it is only when we become unhealthy, either permanently or temporarily, that many people consider it more carefully.

Health

Health has been defined by the World Health Organisation as:

> *A state of complete physical, mental and social wellbeing and not merely the absence of disease or infirmity.*

This definition sums up health very well but there are some additional components that can influence your health, which are considered briefly below.

- The use and misuse of substances such as alcohol, tobacco, medicines and other drugs can have a negative influence. Both smoking and excessive alcohol can have short- and long-term effects on your body.
  - *Smoking* – in the long term this can cause a greater risk of developing serious diseases such as lung cancer, heart disease and chronic **bronchitis**. Smoking is a medically proven danger, which is why, by law, each packet has to carry a government health warning.
  - *Alcohol* – in the short term this can cause drunkenness, with a lack of coordination and vomiting. In the long term it can cause severe damage to the liver, muscles and heart as well as mental illness and damage to the immune system.

A *Smoking is definitely a danger and health risk, which is why warnings have to be printed on all cigarette packaging*

Objectives

Define good health.

Consider the components that combine to affect the health of an individual and their link to physical activity.

Key terms

Bronchitis: inflammation of the air passages between the nose and the lungs.

Prescription drugs: drugs that cannot be bought over the counter but only with a doctor's prescription.

Performance-enhancing drugs: a type of unlawful drug that can help to improve sporting performance.

Athlete's foot: a fungal infection between the toes.

links

This topic is closely linked with pages 60–61 on healthy active lifestyle and is also associated with the healthy schools programme on pages 94–95.

- *Drugs* – these can include illegal drugs such as heroin or marijuana, **prescription drugs** and **performance-enhancing drugs** such as anabolic steroids, which many sportspeople are tempted to take. All drugs are chemical substances that alter the biochemical system when they enter the body so they should only be used under medical supervision.

- Sex education deals with the physical, emotional and social aspects of an individual's development as a male or female.

- Family life education looks at the value and importance of the family as a social institution.

- Safety in different environments, including at home, on the roads, at school and work, and during leisure activities.

- Health-related exercise and the importance of exercise.

- Nutrition is the link between health and diet.

- Personal hygiene, focusing on personal cleanliness; avoidance of disease and social considerations. Factors linked to PE include:
  - *Washing regularly* – especially after physical activity, can help you avoid minor ailments such as **athlete's foot**.
  - *Ceanliness* – a clean kit, which needs to be washed regularly, should be worn for particular activities.

- Environmental aspects include social, physical and economic factors.

- Psychological aspects include mental health, emotional wellbeing and stress.

B   *Showering immediately after taking part in physical activity is essential to help to maintain good levels of personal hygiene*

Activities

1   Drug-taking in sport is all too common, so find out about some recent drug-taking controversy that has occurred in a major sport or event. Find out which particular drug was used and what the possible side effects of using it could be.

2   Find out more about performance-enhancing drugs and find some information regarding performers who have been caught taking them and the action that was then taken against them.

Study tip

It is important to be able to remember the WHO definition of good health as it is often the focus of a question on this topic. This topic is also often linked to the relationship between health and fitness.

5.2 Healthy active lifestyle

There is a clear link between health and **fitness** and combining the two will allow you to live a healthy, active lifestyle, which in turn will increase the quality of life that you are able to enjoy. There is also a clear link with the amount of **exercise** you manage to include in this lifestyle as well.

Good exercise habits

These can be a great help and are quite easy to incorporate into everyday life, for example:

- Do not be driven everywhere, especially not short distances, but walk instead.
- Try to walk for at least part of a journey – get off a bus one stop earlier.
- Use a bicycle as your chosen form of transport.
- Use at least some of the stairs, if they are available, instead of relying on lifts and escalators.
- If you are involved in a lot of **sedentary** work, try to include some opportunities to exercise in your day.

A *Choosing to cycle, instead of being driven, is an excellent way to improve your basic fitness levels*

Objectives

Consider the differences between health and fitness and also the ways in which they are related.

Consider some good exercise habits that could be adopted.

Be aware of the benefits that can be gained through increasing basic exercise levels.

Key terms

Fitness: good health or good condition, especially as the result of exercise and proper nutrition.

Exercise: activity that requires physical or mental exertion, especially when performed to develop or maintain fitness.

Sedentary: sitting down or being physically inactive for long periods of time.

∞ links

These pages link to pages 58–59 and also to the more specific components of fitness on pages 70–71. There is also a link to the various body systems and diet in Chapters 2, 4 and 5.

Activity

Chart how active you are personally in a typical week and look at opportunities you might have to be more active.

Benefits to be gained

If you do improve your exercise and fitness levels, there are real benefits to be gained, such as:

- improving body shape – activity can help to keep body weight down
- relieving stress and tension
- helping you sleep better
- reducing the chances of getting illnesses and diseases
- toning up your body and improving your posture
- helping to improve basic levels of strength, stamina and flexibility.

B *Someone whose job includes manual labour is likely to have higher fitness levels than someone who has a more sedentary job*

Guidelines and effects

How much additional activity someone needs will depend on the individual. You might have a job that involves being on your feet all day or even one that involves quite a lot of manual labour, in which case your needs would be less than someone who has an office job.

- *Physical condition* – are you already quite healthy and active? If so, you might just need to maintain these levels. If not, you might need to look at ways in which you can improve them.
- *Long-term aims* – this is a lifestyle choice and there will not be immediate changes so you must be prepared to increase levels of activity gradually and over a period of time.

There will be short-term effects when you exercise. These are completely normal and include:

- increased heart and breathing rate
- increased body temperature
- reddening of your skin
- a feeling of tiredness or heaviness in some of the muscles you use.

> **Study tip**
>
> You will need to know what is meant by fitness and exercise and be able to link these to the benefits of leading a healthy, active lifestyle, giving examples of how this can be achieved.

5.3 The structure of the skeletal system

■ Functions

The skeletal system has five particular functions, which are linked directly to its structure:

- *Movement* at joints
- *Support* for muscles and vital organs
- *Shape* for maintaining our basic body shape
- *Protection*, such as the skull protecting the brain
- *Blood-cell production* in the bone marrow.

Activity

Make a list of what the skeleton actually protects within the body. Use the diagram below to work out which specific bones protect which organs.

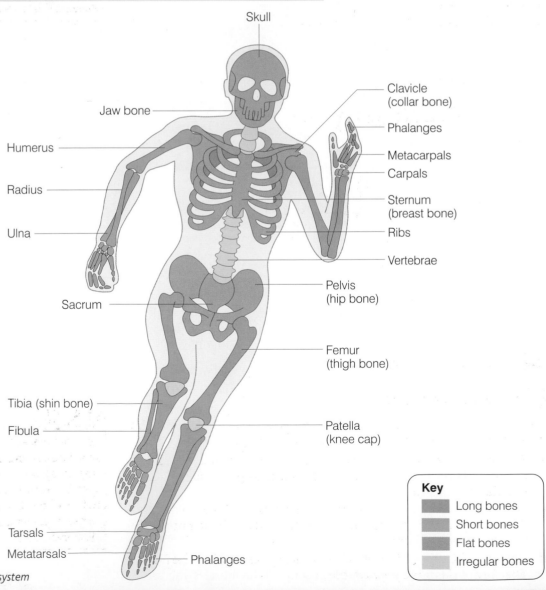

A *The skeletal system*

Key
- Long bones
- Short bones
- Flat bones
- Irregular bones

Bones

The skeletal system (as shown in the diagram) is made up of bones. These fall into the following four categories:

- *Long bones*, such as the femur
- *Short bones*, such as the carpals and tarsals
- *Flat (or plate) bones*, such as the skull
- *Irregular bones*, such as the vertebrae.

Joints

The skeletal system can only allow movement to happen when it is joined up by the muscular system. All movement occurs at **joints**, which fall into these categories:

- *Hinge*, such as the elbow and the knee
- *Ball and socket*, such as the hip and shoulder
- *Pivot*, such as at the wrist
- *Saddle*, such as the thumb
- *Gliding*, such as the bones in the hand
- *Condyloid*, such as the wrist.

⚭ links

This links closely to the role of the skeletal system on pages 64–65 and also to the muscular system as outlined on pages 66–69.

Key terms

Joint: a connection point between two bones where movement occurs.

Quadriceps: the group of four muscles on the upper front of the leg.

Patella: the kneecap.

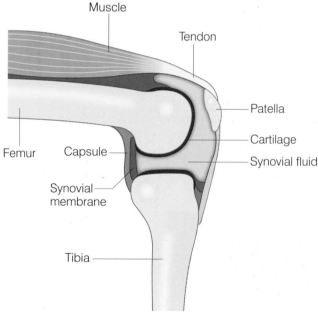

Muscle
Tendon
Patella
Cartilage
Synovial fluid
Femur
Capsule
Synovial membrane
Tibia

B *The knee joint is an example of a hinge joint*

Connective tissue

The diagram of the knee also shows the connective tissue that links the bones to the muscles. There are three types of connective tissue:

- *Tendons* – very strong, non-elastic cords that join the muscles to the bone. They can be seen joining the **quadriceps** muscle to the **patella** on the diagram.
- *Cartilage* – a tough but flexible tissue that acts as a buffer between the bones at joints. This can be seen at the ends of the femur and the tibia in the diagram.
- *Ligaments* – bands of fibre attached to the bones that link the joints. They help to keep the joints stable.

Study tip

You are unlikely to be asked specific questions about the skeletal system or to identify specific joints, but you will need to know how it allows the body to move and its role in protecting vital organs.

5.4 The role of the skeletal system

Although the skeletal system has five distinct functions, the main role to be considered is that of movement, as this is what happens at joints. The amount of movement that does occur differs between different joints.

Joints

- *Freely movable joints* – the majority of joints fall into this category and are known as **synovial**.
- *Slightly movable* – a good example of this is the vertebrae in the spine.
- *Immovable* – there is no movement here, such as the bones that make up the skull.

Movements

There are specific names given to specific movements. The following are the most common of these:

- *Flexion* – the decreasing of an angle at a joint, such as bending the arm at the elbow.
- *Extension* – the opposite movement to flexion where the angle at a joint is increased, such as straightening the arm at the elbow.
- *Abduction* – the movement of a bone or limb away from the midline of the body, such as the first movement of a star jump with the arms and legs.
- *Adduction* – the opposite movement to abduction where the bone or limb moves towards the body, such as the return of the movement of the arms and legs when performing a star jump.

A *When performing this star jump the outward movement of the arms and legs is abduction and the return movement is adduction*

Objectives

Be aware of the role that the skeletal system plays in allowing movement.

Consider the types of movement that are possible because of the skeletal system.

Key terms

Synovial: where bony surfaces are covered by cartilage, connected by ligaments with a joint cavity containing synovial fluid.

Articulation: a movable joint between inflexible parts of the body.

Activity

Perform any normal physical movement and attempt to identify exactly which joints are allowing the movement to take place.

B   *The head turn of a swimmer when breathing is a good example of rotation*

- *Rotation* – a turning action, such as turning your head to the side when breathing in front crawl.

The support function of the skeleton is where the framework of the skeleton connects to the muscles to keep our bodies rigid. It allows **articulation** to take place, which in turn links to the protection function. Our general shape is determined by our skeleton, with muscle size and the body fat then dictating our body type. Red and white blood cells are produced in the bone marrow and mineral salts, such as calcium, are stored in the bones.

Movement and activity

For any movement to occur, there is usually a combination of movements at several joints. Physical activity puts quite a strain on the body and stress on the joints. We need stability and flexibility at the joints to allow complex movements in different directions to take place. We also need to take into account that exercise helps the development of the skeleton in young people at a time when a great deal of growth is also taking place. It is for this reason that adolescents need to make sure that muscular growth does not happen quicker than skeletal growth to avoid injuries occurring.

∞ links

These pages link to many of the other sections as movement is a very complex action, which uses the muscular system on pages 66–69 and the skeletal system on pages 62–63. Other factors, such as age and body shape, also need to be considered.

Study tip

This topic is closely linked to the practical component. You need to be aware of any form of movement required such as physical actions in training, which require specific movements such as the ones identified in this spread.

5.5   The structure of the muscular system

◼ Muscles

The muscular system clearly has to link with the skeletal system in order for movement to occur, as it is the muscles that are attached to the bones that allow this movement. There are over 600 muscles in the body, but you only need to be aware of the major ones involved in the majority of movements and the ones that make up the major muscle groups.

Activity

You can quite easily experience the contraction and relaxation of muscles in action by placing your hand around your upper arm, either side of your biceps and triceps, and bending and straightening your arm at the elbow. You will be able to feel the muscles contract and relax, feeling bigger and smaller.

There are three types of muscle:

1 Skeletal muscles

These are also called 'voluntary muscles' and they make up the majority of the muscles in the body, with the main ones shown on the diagram. It is these muscles that help to give the body its shape. They are called 'voluntary' because they are under your conscious control and only move through a conscious effort.

Objectives

Be aware of the main muscles that make up the muscular system.

Identify the three different types of muscle.

Consider the way in which movement occurs through the link of the muscular system to the skeletal system.

∞ links

This links to the role of the muscular system on pages 68–69, which has to be considered with the structure and role of skeletal system on pages 62–65 as these two body systems are dependent upon each other to allow movement.

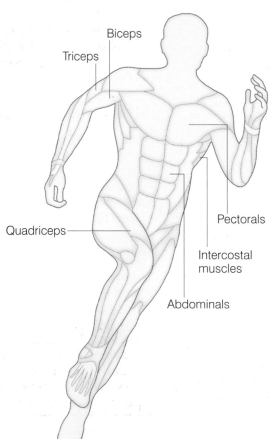
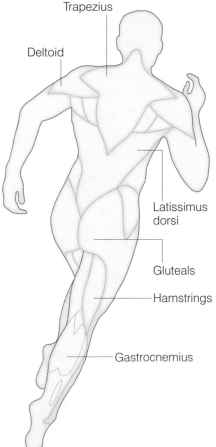

Biceps
Triceps
Quadriceps
Pectorals
Intercostal muscles
Abdominals

Trapezius
Deltoid
Latissimus dorsi
Gluteals
Hamstrings
Gastrocnemius

A *The main skeletal muscles seen from the front and the back*

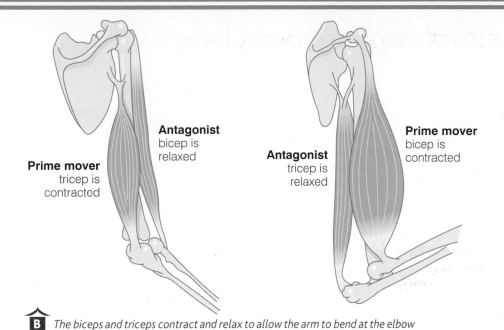

Antagonist
bicep is
relaxed

Prime mover
tricep is
contracted

Antagonist
tricep is
relaxed

Prime mover
bicep is
contracted

B *The biceps and triceps contract and relax to allow the arm to bend at the elbow*

2 Cardiac muscles

These are a form of involuntary muscles as they work automatically and constantly. They are only found in the walls of the heart, working to make sure that the heart is beating consistently.

3 Involuntary muscles

These are muscles that you cannot control, which are found in the walls of the intestines and in the blood vessels. They have to keep contracting to allow crucial body functions to continue.

Muscles and movement

Muscles only provide one type of movement as they can only pull and not push. It is because of this that all muscles work in pairs, with one muscle pulling in one way while the other relaxes, and then vice versa.

The muscle is attached to the bone by a tendon. For movement to take place, one bone stays in place while the other one moves through the action of the **origin** and the **insertion** and the **prime mover** and **antagonist**.

Exercise helps to improve the strength and flexibility of tendons and ligaments, which is important as these are the areas where the greatest amount of stress is applied during movement. They are also very often injured or damaged.

Our muscles always maintain a slight degree of tension as the prime movers and antagonists are working against each other. This is known as 'muscle tone' and it helps with core stability as the main muscles maintain the correct alignment of the spine and pelvis. It is this muscle tone that helps us to maintain a good posture.

Key terms

Origin: the end of the muscle attached to the fixed bone.

Insertion: the end of the muscle attached to the bone that moves.

Prime mover: the muscle that initially contracts to start a movement, also known as the 'agonist'.

Antagonist: the muscle that relaxes to allow a movement to take place.

Study tip

You will not need to identify and name specific muscles but you do need to understand why muscles are arranged in pairs.

5.6 The role of the muscular system

Muscles and movement

The muscular system allows us to move body parts, stabilise joints when movement is happening and protects and keeps vital organs in place while also giving us our individual shape (as it makes up just over 40 per cent of our total body mass).

Muscles fall into separate categories that relate to specific movements:

- *Flexors* – the muscles that bend a limb at a joint by contracting.
- *Extensors* – the muscles that work with and against the flexors and that straighten a limb at a joint by contracting.
- *Adductors* – the muscles that move a limb towards the body.
- *Abductors* – the paired muscles for adductors, which move a limb away from the body.

Muscular contractions

When these muscles do contract, they do so in one of two ways:

- *Isotonic contractions* – these can be **concentric** or **eccentric**.
- *Isometric contractions* – here there is no actual movement of either the limb or the joint because the muscles are working to keep the joint stable.

A *This gymnast is able to maintain her handstand through isometric contractions in her arms*

Objectives

Consider the basic roles that the muscular system fulfils.

Be aware of the particular movements that various muscles can allow.

Consider specific muscles and muscle groups, and the major movements they are responsible for.

Key terms

Concentric: when the muscle shortens (it also tends to bulge, such as the biceps in the arm).

Eccentric: when the muscle gradually lengthens and returns to its normal length and shape.

Activity

Place your left hand around your right forearm with your right arm out straight. Clench your right fist and you will feel the isometric contraction in your forearm.

∞ links

It is important to be aware of the location of the muscles mentioned by checking their location on pages 66–67 and to consider which muscles and muscle groups need to be concentrated on for specific training programmes (Chapter 6).

Major muscles and movement functions

The following muscles are considered in their pairs and muscle groups, also considering the major movements they allow:

- *Biceps and triceps* – are mainly involved in any movements of the arms, especially at the elbow including any type of throwing movement, such as a javelin or a ball and a smash at tennis, badminton or volleyball.

- *Hamstrings and quadriceps* – are involved in the movements of the legs including any kicking movement, such as kicking a football, as well as running movements, especially sprinting and jogging.

B *Alex Morgan about to strike for the USA. Kicking a football requires the contraction and relaxation of the quadriceps and hamstrings.*

- *Abdominals* – these are made up of three major muscles that allow movement around the stomach and waist. These are very important for keeping the body straight and upright in a variety of movements as well as specifically when doing exercises such as sit-ups.

- *Pectorals* – these allow the arm to be raised at the shoulders, so would be involved in the tennis drive, shot put and all of the swimming strokes.

- *Gastrocnemius* – these are involved in initial movements of the legs, specifically running and the take-off phase of any type of jump.

Very few movements involve only one set of muscular contractions. Most movements involve a variety of movements that are linked together. A pole-vaulter, for example, would be involved in a very complex number of movements involving all of the major muscle groups.

Study tip

You may need to know the contribution that the muscular system makes to muscular endurance and also its relationship with flexibility/ suppleness.

5.7 Components of fitness

Strength

This can be defined simply as 'the ability to bear weight' but strength can also be subdivided into three distinct and separate categories:

- *Dynamic strength* – this is the strength a sportsperson needs to support their own body weight over a prolonged period of time, or to be able to apply force against some type of object.
- *Explosive strength* – this is strength used in one short sharp, burst or movement.
- *Static strength* – this is the greatest amount of strength that can be applied to an immovable object.

Most activities require a degree of all of these types of strength. For example, a rugby player needs static strength to push against the other pack in a scrum, explosive strength to take a tap penalty and then sprint and dynamic strength to last the whole of an 80-minute match. It is possible to improve all aspects of strength through strength-training programmes.

Objectives

Consider fitness capability in terms of the various components of fitness.

Consider each of the separate components of fitness.

Consider the ways in which these components can be affected by training.

Hand grip dynamometer

This is a test to measure grip or forearm muscle strength. The device is squeezed with maximum isometric effort for 5 seconds with no other body movement allowed. The best of two trials are then compared against a values table, giving scores ranging from 'excellent' to 'very poor' and·linked to both males and females. However, this is not a valid test of general strength as the forearms do not necessarily represent the strength of other muscles.

Speed

This is the ability to move all or parts of the body as quickly as possible. It is a combination of **reaction time** and **movement time**. It is possible to work on improving some aspects of speed by increasing strength, for example, but some factors are **inherent**, such as the percentage of fast twitch muscle fibres, which can give greater speed.

Power

This is the combination of the maximum amount of speed with the maximum amount of strength. Power is closely linked to explosive strength. It is also something that cannot be maintained for long periods of time, but it can be improved through strength training.

Standing broad jump

This is also sometimes called the 'standing long jump' and measures the explosive power of the legs. A non-slip floor is needed for take-off and a soft mat for the landing. The performer stands behind a marked line with feet apart and then performs a two-footed take-off and landing. It is best to swing the arms and bend the knees to provide the maximum amount of forward drive in the jump. The distance travelled is measured. Three attempts are allowed and the results attained are compared to a values table.

links

These pages must be considered closely with training in Chapter 6 as most of these factors can be improved by using a suitable training programme.

Vertical jump

This is also known as the 'Sargent jump', measuring the height of a jump. The performer stands by a wall and reaches up as high a possible with the hand closest to the wall. Keeping their feet flat on the ground, the highest point reached is recorded. The performer then stands away from the wall and jumps up vertically as high as possible using both arms and legs to help their momentum. They then have to attempt to touch the wall at the highest point of the jump. The difference between the standing reach height and jump height is recorded, with the best of three attempts allowed.

Double Award

■ Cardiovascular endurance

This is also often referred to as 'stamina' and is the ability of the heart and lungs to keep operating efficiently during an endurance event. As with many of the other components, this factor can also be improved through training.

Cooper 12-minute run

This test is taken on a 400-metre track which is marked out at 100-metre intervals. A warm-up should take place before the start and the performer then runs as far as possible in 12 minutes. The total distance is recorded to the nearest 100 metres. This result can be compared to previous attempts and it can also be compared to a values table set against age and gender.

Double Award

Multi-stage fitness test

This is described and covered on page 89.

■ Flexibility

This is often called 'suppleness' and refers to the range of movement around a joint. Increased flexibility can help:

- make a performance more effective and more efficient
- reduce the chances of injury
- improve body posture.

It is possible to improve the levels of flexibility by regularly performing stretching exercises. Levels do tend to decrease with age so this is even more important as you get older.

Sit and reach test

This tests the flexibility of the lower back and hamstring muscles and involves the performer sitting on the floor with legs straight out ahead. The feet (with shoes removed) are placed flat against a box, shoulder width apart and both knees are held flat against the floor. With the hands on top of each other and palms facing down, the performer reaches forward as far as possible. After three practice reaches, the fourth is held for at least two seconds, the distance is recorded and compared to a values table.

Double Award

Activity

It is very likely that you will be asked to plan and even perform some form of exercise training programme, so you need to consider which of the factors identified in this unit are most important to you and which need to be improved upon. Try to rank order all of them and think of ways you could improve them through training.

Key terms

Reaction time: how quickly you are able to respond to something or some form of stimulus.

Movement time: how quickly a performer can carry out an actual movement.

Inherent: something you are born with.

B *This trampolinist is able to perform moves effectively as he has good levels of flexibility*

Study tip

It is important to be aware of what each of these components of fitness is, being able to give a concise definition for each of them. You should also be able to identify how each factor could be improved.

kerboodle

5.8 Skill-related factors of fitness

These are factors affecting your levels of fitness that are specifically related to skill levels, which means they are therefore factors that you are able to do something about. All skills can be improved through practice, but they may also need some degree of training, making use of the components of fitness.

■ Agility

This is a combination of flexibility and speed and is the ability to move quickly, changing direction and speed whenever possible. Clearly, this is something that can be improved and it is an important factor in many activities.

Double Award

Illinois agility test

This makes use of marking cones, a measuring tape and timing gates. The performer has to lie down on their front (head towards the start line) with hands by their shoulders. When told to start, they have to get up as quickly as possible and run around the course of set out cones to the finishing line where the watch is then stopped. The course is 10 metres by 5 metres with four cones marked out at the start, finish and two turning points. Another four cones are placed down the centre an equal distance apart with each cone in the centre spaced 3.3 metres apart. The final score can be compared against a rating scores table.

■ Balance

This is the ability to maintain a given posture in static and dynamic situations and to be able to stay level and stable. This is something that is very important in some specific activities, such as gymnastics, but it is also an important factor for all performers who need to change balance positions throughout a performance. Balance is very closely linked to agility as you have to be in a stable position before you are able to change direction quickly.

Double Award

Stork stand

This is a test of the ability to maintain a state of balance and is very simple to perform. Start by standing on both feet with hands on hips and lift one leg. Place the toes of that foot against the knee of the other. Then you have to raise the heel of your standing leg, standing on your toes and balance for as long as possible without either letting the heel touch the ground or the other foot moving away from the knee. The total time the balance is maintained is recorded and compared against a values table.

Objectives

Consider the ways in which skill-related factors contribute to fitness and effective performance.

Consider specific skill-related factors.

Be aware of how these factors interrelate with each other and also with the components of fitness.

∞ links

These factors must be considered together with those identified on pages 70–71 as well as skill acquisition on pages 74–75. They must also be considered in relation to training in Chapter 6.

A *This hockey player needs to maintain her balance while dribbling in order to be able to change direction quickly*

Key terms

Synchronise: an adjustment that causes something to occur at the same time.

Ambidextrous: the ability to use both hands with equal levels of skill.

Coordination

This is the ability to link all the parts of a movement into one efficient smooth movement and is the ability to be able to control the body during physical activity. It is important to have good hand–eye coordination as this is the ability to **synchronise** the movement of the hands and eyes for movements such as catching a ball, using a hockey stick or some sort of racket. This can be extended to foot–eye coordination for football players. Most sports performers will find that they have higher levels of coordination on their dominant side and a few people are **ambidextrous**.

Alternate hand throw

Also known as the 'alternate hand wall toss test'. A mark is placed a certain distance from a wall (usually about two metres) and the performer stands behind the line and faces the wall. The ball is thrown from one hand in an underarm action against the wall and caught with the opposite hand. The ball is then thrown back against the wall, and caught again with the initial hand. This test can continue for a nominated number of attempts or for a set time period.

Reaction time

This is the time taken for the body, or part of the body, to respond to a stimulus. This can be divided into two specific cases:

- *Simple reaction time* – this is where someone must react to something as it happens. For example, a sprinter at the start of a race has to react to the sound of the gun going off in order to record their fastest time.
- *Choice reaction time* – this occurs when someone is able to size up a situation and then decide when they are going to react. For example, a footballer has to decide the best time to make a tackle.

The factor of speed is clearly important so improving speed is likely to help improve your reaction times as well.

Ruler drop test

All that is needed for this test is a one metre ruler, held by an assistant between the outstretched index finger and thumb of the performer's dominant hand. The performer's thumb should be level with the zero centimetre line of the ruler. The performer has to catch the ruler as soon as possible after it has been dropped.

Timing

Timing is the ability to coincide movements in relation to external factors. It combines decision-making, reaction time and coordination to be able to perform some movement or action. Making contact with any sort of ball or object requires very good timing if the contact and end result are to be the best possible.

B *This sprinter needs excellent reaction times to be able to make the fastest possible start*

5.9 Skill acquisition

Skill

Skill is using knowledge or expertise to succeed efficiently and effectively in achieving a particular objective and ability, which has been acquired by training. Skills can be considered in two categories:

- *Basic skills* – these are often fairly simple and straightforward, such as being able to throw, catch, run, jump and hit an object. It is important to be able to perform basic skills with some ease before attempting higher levels.

- *Complex skills* – these are skills that take quite a long time to learn as they involve high levels of coordination and control. Higher level skills will also be very sport-specific as particular activities have different skills unique to that activity.

Objectives

Be aware of what skills are and how they can be acquired and developed.

Be aware of the different types of guidance that may be available.

Be aware of the different types of feedback available and the types of practice that can be used.

Activity

Choose one activity that you regularly take part in and make a list of the basic skills and complex skills that you need to apply.

A *Performing the pole vault requires a coordinated combination of several complex skills*

Types of skill

These are considered to be in two categories:

- *Open skills* – these occur in situations that are constantly changing, such as any invasion game activity where the environment around the performer is constantly changing and skills may have to be adapted according to the demands of the game.

- *Closed skills* – these occur in situations that are constant and unchanging so they are not affected by the sporting environment, such as performing a trampoline routine.

Types of guidance

In order to acquire skill, performers often need additional guidance, which can be given in the following ways:

- *Visual* – seeing a demonstration, example or even watching their own performance played back.

∞ links

This has to be considered in conjunction with pages 70–73, as well as training in Chapter 6. However, it will also be a specific aspect of Chapter 6 for Double Award entries.

- *Verbal* – being told what needs to be done, what went well or what needs improvement through constructive criticism.
- *Manual* – some performers can be physically guided through something, such as being helped with support with a vault.

B   *Gymnast Kristian Thomas is receiving verbal feedback from coach Andrey Popov in order to help improve his performance*

Types of feedback

A performer finds out how good their performance was through **knowledge of results** and also **knowledge of performance**. The most common ways are:

- *Intrinsic* – this is sensed or felt by the performer while they are actually performing.
- *Extrinsic* – this comes from sources other than the performer themselves, such as sounds or things they can see.

Types of practice

These are the ways a performer tries to gain skills that they have particularly identified. There are four main ways to do this:

- *Whole* – a complete performance is carried out with all aspects of the performance covered.
- *Part* – complex skills are broken down into parts and each part is practised.
- *Fixed* – a set session or aspect is concentrated upon.
- *Variable* – a combination of all of the above.

Key terms

Knowledge of results: this is a form of terminal feedback at the end of a performance and could be as simple as winning or losing.

Knowledge of performance: this relates to how well the performance was carried out rather than just the end result.

Study tip

You may not be examined on this aspect of the specification as it only applies to Double Award candidates but it is important applied knowledge about how to be an effective performer.

Chapter summary

5

In this chapter you have learnt:

✔ what good health is and how it is possible to achieve and maintain it

✔ what the differences are between health and fitness and how they can also combine

✔ how the skeletal system is structured and the major bones that make up the system

✔ the various roles that the skeletal system performs

✔ how the muscular system is structured, the functions the system performs and how movement occurs through the link with the skeletal system

✔ to identify the various components of fitness and how they can be improved by training

✔ what skills are and how skill acquisition can be improved and developed.

Revision questions

1 Which of the following would be considered to be a sedentary job?
   a Construction worker
   b Secretary
   c PE teacher
   d Fitness instructor

2 Give a general definition of what good health is.

3 What short-term effects can drinking too much alcohol have?

4 Explain two good exercise habits that you could easily use daily.

5 Describe two benefits that can be gained by exercising regularly.

6 Give five different functions that the skeletal system performs.

7 What is a tendon and what function does it perform?

8 What function does cartilage perform and where would it be found?

9 What is meant by the following four movements?
   a Flexion
   b Extension
   c Abduction
   d Adduction

10 Name the three different types of muscle.

11 Why are muscles always arranged in pairs?

12 What is meant by an isometric contraction?

13 Describe one action that the quadriceps and hamstrings would combine together to allow.

14 What is agility a combination of?

15 What is the difference between an open and closed skill?

16 What is the difference between intrinsic and extrinsic feedback?

6 Training

Aims

✔ Understand and define the factors that affect the ability to train.

✔ Understand how to apply these factors in a practical way.

✔ Be aware of the safety precautions and requirements.

✔ Consider individual needs and requirements.

✔ Look in some detail at some specific training methods that are available.

✔ Be able to match training methods to particular activities.

This chapter focuses specifically on training and considers the different types of training that are available to individuals. Some form of training is essential for all performers to be able to improve all aspects of their performance. It is equally essential to make sure that any training taking place is the correct type, is effective and is safe.

The whole point of carrying out training is to bring about a change. This may be a physiological one, directly affecting one of the body systems, such as the muscular system. It is because of this that you must be aware of what these effects will be and how to make sure that you are concentrating on improving the ones that you need. You may also be trying to improve specific skills relating to an activity, which can also be incorporated.

You are likely to be asked to plan out an individual training programme – this may even be an essential part of your course if you are being entered for the Double Award.

6.1 Principles of training: specificity and progression

Training takes place in order to improve ability and capability to take part in an activity more effectively. This requires an actual change in the body, specifically the body systems, so that a physical change takes place. Knowledge of the body systems, such as the muscular system and cardiovascular system, is essential as these will be affected by training and are the systems particularly targeted for improvement.

The aspects of training apply to all forms of training so it is essential that they are correctly incorporated into any training programme so that it can be as successful as possible.

It is important to know both **how** and **why** training is able to make these changes and also to be aware of some basic guidelines to make sure that you are carrying out training safely. This is why you must be aware of thresholds of training that guide how much training should take place, how hard and for how long. This will be linked to current fitness levels as each individual has a specific threshold that in turn is linked to training zones.

Specificity

If you were an endurance athlete, such as a marathon runner, you would make sure that your training suited that particular activity, so you would train to increase your levels of endurance. You would also need to make sure that distance running was included in your training so that you were actually practising your event. Individuals are different and will respond differently to the same method of training, so this must be taken into account as well as the specific demands each activity will have. A weightlifter is more likely to train specifically to increase strength as opposed to other aspects of **specificity**.

A *It is important for weightlifters to train to increase the strength in their arms*

Objectives

Understand the ways in which different factors affect the capacity to train.

Understand and define these factors.

Key terms

Specificity: training that is particularly suited to a particular sport or activity.

⊙⊙ links

Ensure that you are familiar with the cardiovascular, skeletal and muscular systems on pages 42–43 and 62–69, as well as aspects of training on pages 82–83.

◼ Progression

Any training you do must be increased gradually as your body adjusts to the different demands that are being made on it. If you keep the levels the same then no real **progression** will happen, but you must also make sure that you do not try to do too much too soon as this could result in an injury or muscle damage.

Another factor you must be aware of is that of **plateauing**, which is where you progress to a certain level and then get stuck there and are unable to move on. If you know this is likely to happen, you can prepare yourself mentally and keep yourself motivated enough to keep going.

Activity

Hold a bag of sugar in the palm of your hand with your arm straight out and the palm facing upwards. Keep it there with your arm straight and you will soon feel the muscles that are affected. If you wanted to improve the time that you can hold out your arm, you would have to train specifically to increase the strength in those muscles.

Key terms

Progression: where training is increased gradually as the body adjusts to the increased demands being made on it.

Plateauing: where progress seems to halt within a training programme and it takes some time to move on to the next level.

Study tip

Use the acronym SPORT to remember the principles of training:

Specificity
Progression
Overload
Reversibility
Tedium – varying the way you train can reduce this!

B *Progressive training strengthens our muscles*

kerboodle

6.2 Principles of training: overload and reversibility

■ Overload

There are different ways in which you can **overload** your body and these are usually known by the acronym **FIT**.

Frequency

This means increasing the number of training sessions. A top performer will take part in some form of training every day, but when you start training you must consider progression and make sure that you increase gradually.

Intensity

This means increasing the actual amount of activity you are including in one session, such as increasing weights (if you are using them) or increasing the number of exercises, such as sit-ups.

Time

This is also known as 'duration' and means increasing the actual amount of time you spend taking part in the training session. Increasing this adds overload as well.

■ Reversibility

Progression will help you to move forward but **reversibility** is the opposite effect. If you stop or decrease your training, then all the good work you have put in will be lost. Top performers calculate that if they have to stop training for a certain period of time then it takes up to three times that period to get back to the state they were in previously. It is clear that gains made are definitely lost at a faster rate than they are initially achieved.

■ Combination training

Very few performers just carry out one specific form of training, but they carry out a range and variety of training. A decathlete has to train for 10 specific activities – the 1,500-metre run requires endurance training, while the shot put requires strength training. Not all sports performers have such extremes as this but many games players carry out some basic endurance training, such as a training run, and muscular endurance work, using weight-training machines in a fitness suite, so that they can improve their all-round levels of fitness.

> ### Objectives
>
> Understand how to apply these factors in a practical way.
>
> Understand the safe and correct way to put together a training programme.

> ### Key terms
>
> **Overload:** making the body work harder than normal in order to improve it.
>
> **FIT:** frequency, intensity and time are ways to make the body work harder.
>
> **Reversibility:** if training stops then the effects gained can be lost too.

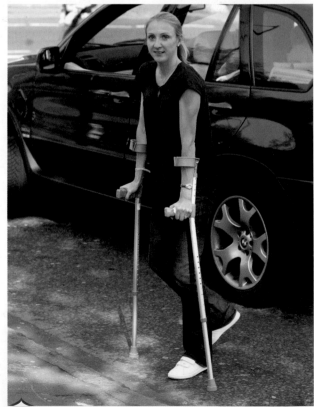

A *Paula Radcliffe recovering from injury. Unexpected injury may mean that you are no longer able to continue training or competing. It may take some time to regain previous fitness levels.*

B *Tennis player Andy Murray added a great deal of strength training to his endurance training, in order to be able to 'bulk up' to gain increased power*

Activity

1 Try to work out a basic training programme that would suit you best. Remember to consider **specificity** when initially planning, the rate of **progression** you are hoping for, the ways you will set **overload** targets, and try to come up with some ways to avoid **tedium**!

Activity

2 Plan, put together and then evaluate a specific training programme. This may be an important feature for someone taking the double-award qualification.

Double Award

Safety

This is an important factor to consider as the aspects of training require you to push your body beyond its normal limits in order to be able to improve. You should always complete a thorough warm-up before each session, as well as a warm-down afterwards. You should be well aware of any specific safety requirements for a particular training method, such as having spotters when using freestanding weights.

∞ links

Make sure that you are aware of the cardiovascular and muscular systems pages 42–43 and 66–69, as these will be directly affected by applying overload.

∞ links

Be aware of safety precautions and considerations on pages 144–145 and warm-ups and warm-downs on pages 82–83.

Study tip

You are likely to be asked for examples to explain the aspect you are considering. Use your own experiences and consider the major muscles or muscle groups that would be affected.

6.3   Aspects of training

When you are fully aware of the principles of training, you can use these effectively in a specific training programme. All training programmes and training sessions usually have specific parts or phases, which are the aspects of training:

- Warm-up
- Fitness or exercise phase
- Skills or team-play phase
- Warm-down (also known as 'cool-down').

There may be times when training is carried out individually, such as for a marathon runner, but in many team games it is often carried out with a group of people.

Warm-up

All training sessions should start with a warm-up and it is important that it should be carried out before any form of physical activity for the following reasons:

- To prepare the body for the activity and increase blood flow, also allowing you to become psychologically prepared.
- To reduce the possibility of being injured, especially the chance of some form of muscle injury. Cold muscles are more prone to damage to the fibres and tendons.

Warm-ups should really be designed to be specific to either the activity you are preparing to take part in or to complement the overall training method you are about to start. The following would usually be included within your warm-up:

- A pulse raiser of some sort of continuous movement, light jogging or gentle exercise. This should be just enough to make sure that you increase the heart rate, breathing rate and the body temperature in a balanced way, but do not overdo it.
- Light exercises, stretches/flexibility movements, which specifically prepare the main muscles, muscle groups and areas of the body that are going to be used. Some gentle mobility movements are good.

Objectives

Consider how to design training to be most effective.

Be aware of what should be included within a training session.

Be able to cater for individual needs.

∞ links

This links to pulse rates and the respiratory system on pages 36–43, as well as skill factors on pages 72–73.

A *Brad Barritt of the England rugby team warming up. Some mobility/flexibility exercises are essential before starting any activity.*

Fitness phase

This is where you concentrate on the aspect of fitness specifically identified and that is most appropriate for your particular physical activity. There would probably be an endurance exercise included here and the principle of overload may well be used. It may be that you include a variety of exercises if you are using circuit training as the method, for example.

Skill phase

If you are training for a team activity, the skill phase is where you would link with the rest of the team or group. However, you could also practise the individual skills that you need for your particular activity.

B *Practising team skills are essential in order to improve*

Warm-down

Rather than just stopping at the end of your session, you should end the session gradually, taking some light exercise to help with your recovery and to remove **lactic acid** and other waste materials so that you are not sore or stiff later.

Thresholds of training

As well as matching personal needs, training sessions must also be designed to suit each individual need. This could include factors such as age, experience, existing fitness levels, actual ability levels and the level of motivation. A simple way to calculate an individual **training threshold** is by using the standard formula of MHR (maximum heart rate) = 220 minus age. This means that for a 16-year-old the MHR should be 204 ($220 - 16 = 204$).

Closely linked to this are the particular **training zones** that apply, which all link to your MHR:

■ Training zone = 80–90% of MHR

■ Aerobic zone = 60–80% of MHR.

6.4 Circuit training

Circuit training is one of the most common forms of training and it is popular because it is easy to set up and very flexible.

Setting up

Circuit training uses a variety of different exercises or activities that are commonly known as **stations**, with a normal circuit consisting of anything from 6 to 10 or 12 activities. These are some guidelines that should be considered when setting your circuit up:

- Each station should be clearly marked and the exercise or activity should be identified. Ideally, this would include a diagram of how the exercise should be properly performed.

- Exercises/activities should be demonstrated and even practised to make sure that they are being performed correctly.

- There should be a variety of exercises and activities within the circuit, which are carefully varied. Similar exercises, such as sit-ups, leg-raises and abdominal crunches, should be spread out so that they do not follow each other.

- There should always be a recovery period built in to the circuit so that there are periods of work and periods of rest.

Objectives

Consider the types of circuit that can be used.

Look at the types of benefit that can be gained.

Consider some of the content that could be included in a planned circuit.

∞ links

This links to principles and aspects of training on pages 80–83.

A *This circuit clearly shows the different stations that could be used in a typical school gym*

Fitness circuit

This would primarily be aimed at increasing general fitness and would include a variety of different exercises designed to increase cardiovascular fitness or strength in specific muscles or muscle groups. The type of exercises you could use include the following:

- Press-ups
- Squat thrusts
- Skipping
- Squats
- Triceps dips
- Star jumps
- Burpees (squat thrusts followed by a star jump, then back into a squat thrust again)
- Trunk curls
- Shuttle runs
- Step-ups and sit-ups
- Running on the spot
- Sprint starts (in press-up position with legs positioned for a sprint start, quickly switching the right and left legs over to the front and back position).

The main advantage of using this type of circuit is that you need little or no specialist equipment and it can easily be carried out in a standard school gym or sports hall.

Skills circuit

This would also make use of stations, but these exercises are particularly aimed at developing certain skills that are vital in a particular activity. These are usually used by games players where individual skills can be practised, such as passing a ball against a wall and dribbling in and out of cones for soccer or basketball.

Activities

1   Use between 6 to 10 of the exercises listed to create your own fitness circuit. Make sure you think about the order of the exercises so that you do not have similar ones following on from each other.

2   Choose a sport and think of some particular skills that would be necessary for this sport. Add two skills activities to the general fitness circuit you planned in the previous activity.

Running the circuit

There are different ways in which circuits can be organised and run, but these are some of the most common:

- *Timed circuits* – there is a set time for the exercises, completing as many as possible in this time. A rest period follows immediately afterwards for recovery. The times can be the same or either can be longer or shorter.
- *Fixed load* – each particular station is labelled with the exact amount of work that must be done, without any particular time limit. For example, 15 press-ups followed by 30 sit-ups.
- *Varied laps* – most circuits consist of one or more laps. These can be exactly the same, increased work and reduced rest (or vice-versa), or you can have 'sprint laps' where a whole lap is completed very quickly with perhaps 10 seconds of work and only 3 seconds of rest before you move on to the next activity.

B   *These pictures show how to perform the stages of a burpee*

Key terms

Stations: particular areas where types of exercise are set up or performed.

Laps: the number of times each set of stations is performed.

Study tip

Questions are often asked about the specific advantages or disadvantages of circuit training. The ease of setting up is a good example of an advantage, while the need for a large space is a good example of a disadvantage.

6.5 Weight training

Benefits

Weight training is primarily used to improve some aspect of muscular strength, which could also include power and endurance. It may also have benefits by:

- improving muscular strength
- increasing muscle size or bulk
- improving **muscle tone**
- assisting recovery after injury.

Organising effective sessions

Just about all activities require some form of strength so some degree of weight training is likely to benefit all performers. It is because of this that there has been a rapid growth in specialised weight-training equipment and facilities.

A   *This type of specialist weight-training equipment is now readily available for all sports performers*

Effective weight training involves the application of the principle of overload so that the muscles are actually stressed to make them adapt to become both bigger and stronger and therefore more efficient. Two terms are particularly relevant to weight training:

- **Repetitions** – the number of times you actually move the weights, so one bicep curl equals one repetition.
- **Sets** – the number of times you carry out a particular weight activity, so each time you complete your repetitions of the bicep curl, you have completed one set.

B   *One completed movement of this bicep curl equals one repetition. The number you complete in one go would be one set.*

The different ways you make use of repetitions and sets will affect the different aspects of strength you might be training for. For example:

- to increase muscular strength you would work on having three sets of six repetitions at near maximum weight
- to increase muscular endurance you would perform at least three sets of between 20 and 30 repetitions at about 40–60 per cent of maximum weight
- to increase power you would complete at least three sets of 10–15 repetitions, performed at speed, at about 60–80 per cent of maximum weight.

Types of weight training

The basic ways to carry out weight training are either by using free-standing weights or by using specialist weight-training equipment.

Free-standing weights

Free-standing weights have to be placed onto bars and equipment in order for them to be used, usually on short or long bars. These are often used by people who specifically want to increase strength as it is easier to add more weight. Also, it is possible to buy your own set of weights for a reasonable price and set up your own weight training area by just adding a bench. One of the main issues and possible drawbacks relating to using free-standing weights is the safety consideration, as weights can be dropped. If weights become too heavy to lift they can fall on you, so you should always work with at least one training partner.

Specialist weight-training equipment

These are the types of machines found in specialist gyms, leisure centres and private clubs. The weights are fixed within the machine and are usually selected by placing pins in selected slots. These machines are much safer to use because there is far less chance of accident or injury, even if the weights are too heavy.

C This leg-press machine is a safe and convenient way to carry out specific weight training

6.6 Further training methods

Continuous training

This is any type of training that keeps the heart rate, and therefore the pulse rate, high over a sustained period of time. This can be achieved by taking part in any of the following:

- Running/jogging
- Cycling
- Swimming
- Exercise sessions, such as aerobics.

One of the most popular ways of carrying out continuous training is through using a specific machine such as a treadmill, exercise bike or cross trainer. These machines are widely available in gyms and leisure centres. This is a good form of all-round exercise and very popular for many games players.

Interval training

This is training that has periods of work and periods of rest, with variations of the two. When working, the heart rate needs to be at a high training zone level and during rest it should drop down into the aerobic zone. The two most common forms of this type of training are:

- *Long-interval training* – work periods of between 15 seconds to 3 minutes at about 80–85 per cent of maximum, with corresponding rest periods for recovery. This is a good method for games players and middle-distance athletes.
- *Short-interval training* – short periods of work, no more than 15 seconds but at maximum levels, with a realistic recovery time, possibly up to 2 minutes. This is a good method for racket sports players or sprinters.

Fartlek training

This is a Swedish word meaning 'speed play'. It is a form of interval training that can include walking, brisk walking, jogging and fast steady running.

Objectives

Be aware of other forms of training that are available.

Match training methods to particular activities.

Key terms

Shuttle runs: running backwards and forwards across a set distance.

Aerobic exercise: exercise carried out using a supply of oxygen.

∞ **links**

This links to aspects of training on pages 82–83.

A *This cross trainer is an ideal way to carry out continuous training*

Continuous shuttle run

This is the 'multi-stage fitness test' and is also commonly known as the 'bleep test'. Although it was primarily designed to be a test, it has quickly been adopted as a training method as well. This would be a form of continuous training as it involves carrying out a series of 20-metre **shuttle runs** in time with an electronic bleep that speeds up every minute.

Altitude training

This is where some sort of **aerobic exercise** is carried out at higher altitudes where the air is less dense and oxygen levels are low with less pressure of oxygen. Using this method allows an actual physiological change to occur, which increases the oxygen-carrying capacity of the blood. It is a popular method used by long-distance runners and, increasingly, many football and rugby teams.

Double Award

Activity

Take the 'multi-stage fitness test' and see which level you can achieve. If possible, take the test again later in your course to see what progress you have made.

∞ **links**

For the effects altitude training might have upon the respiratory and cardiovascular systems see pages 36–37 and 42–43.

Study tip

You should be able to match up a particular training method to the specific activity for which it would be the most suitable.

B *This runner is training at altitude in order to improve her performance when she later runs at sea level*

6 O₂

In this chapter you have learnt:

✔ why training is necessary and the benefits that can be gained through making use of it

✔ the types of training that are available and the various advantages and disadvantages of each

✔ how to put together a specific training programme that is going to be safe and effective.

Revision questions

1 Which of the following principles of training might actually have a bad effect on you?
   a Overload
   b Progression
   c Reversibility
   d Specificity

2 Explain what the following terms mean with reference to training:
   a Specificity
   b Overload

3 What does the acronym SPORT stand for?

4 What does the acronym FIT stand for?

5 Explain two reasons why you should carry out a warm-up before starting a training programme.

6 What do you understand by the term 'combination training'? How might this suit a person taking part in a game activity of your choice?

7 What is your particular maximum heart rate? What would be your individual training zone and aerobic zone?

8 Describe two advantages and two disadvantages of choosing circuit training as a particular method of training.

9 Choose two exercises or activities you would include in a circuit and explain why. What specific muscle groups or body system would each one affect?

10 If you were taking part in weight training, what would be meant by 'repetitions' and 'sets'?

11 Describe a specific safety consideration you would have to take into account if you were taking part in a particular form of weight training.

12 Explain the difference between continuous training and interval training. Which training method would you recommend for a long-distance runner?

7 School and physical education

Aims

✔ Understand the reasons why PE is taught in schools and what makes up a PE programme.

✔ Have an overview and outline of the National Healthy Schools Programme.

✔ Understand the range, variety and provision of extra-curricular provisions.

This chapter focuses on the role the school plays in providing opportunities for young people to become aware and educated about the value of taking part in regular physical activity.

Taking part in PE lessons is something you will have been doing since your first days in school. From the time you started Key Stage 3 you will have been taught in timetabled lessons by trained PE teachers. There are many reasons why PE has been developed within the school curriculum and there are now many initiatives in place that puts PE at the forefront in raising the basic health and fitness levels of young people, encouraging them to eat healthily and lead healthy, active lifestyles. The benefits of this are explored in this chapter and it is important that the contents of this chapter are considered together as they are the basis for preparing an individual to establish good habits and a good lifestyle to continue into later life.

7.1 National Curriculum requirements

Each subject taught in school is part of the National Curriculum. It is either a core subject, such as English, mathematics and science, or a foundation subject, such as PE.

The influence of PE in school is thought to be one of the major factors that influences the activity levels of young people as it can shape attitudes and behaviour in the future.

Why is PE offered in schools?

The main reason is that it is a legal requirement (since an Act of Parliament in 1947) because PE is a compulsory subject, but there are other reasons put forward as well:

- To improve health and fitness levels.
- To provide a balance within subjects taught, as it is primarily a practical subject.
- To prepare young people to take part in physical activity when they leave school.
- To provide approved qualifications in line with other subjects (e.g. GCSE and GCE).
- To reflect the importance and value of sport and physical activity in society.

Schools have different ways in which PE is actually made available, such as:

- timetabled PE lessons
- **extra-curricular** provision
- clubs and team practice sessions
- sports performance awards
- links with local clubs and outside visits or visitors.

> **Objectives**
>
> Understand the reasons why PE is included and taught in schools.
>
> Be aware of what should be provided in a PE programme.

> **Key terms**
>
> **Extra-curricular:** an activity that takes place out of timetabled lessons, such as lunchtimes or after school.
>
> **Cross-curricular:** linking with other subjects taught in school.

A These young people are taking part in a compulsory, timetabled PE lesson

> **links**
>
> See the health advantages of taking part in exercise on pages 58–61, as well as the role of extra-curricular provision on pages 96–97 and the increased use of ICT in sport on pages 150–151.

Aspects of PE are not only delivered within PE lessons, but can also be covered in other subject areas in a **cross-curricular** way. There is a strong link with science when studying physiology, and ICT is increasingly being used in many practical applications.

What does the National Curriculum consist of?

A revised National Curriculum was introduced in 2008 when the Key Stage 3 provision was revised and all PE provision was placed in the following categories:

- *Group 1* – outwitting opponents, as in game activities.
- *Group 2* – accurate replication of actions, phrases and sequences, as in gymnastic activities.
- *Group 3* – exploring and communicating ideas, concepts and emotions, as in dance activities.
- *Group 4* – performing at maximum levels in relation to speed, height, distance, strength or accuracy, as in athletic activities.
- *Group 5* – identifying and solving problems to overcome challenges of an adventurous nature, as in lifesaving, personal survival in swimming and outdoor and adventurous activities.
- *Group 6* – exercising safely and effectively to improve health and wellbeing, as in fitness and health activities.

Activity

Find out how many PE activities are offered in your school in curriculum time.

links

Health and safety and issues are considered in more depth on pages 144–145.

B   *Dance is an essential part of the PE provision in schools and is an ideal way to express ideas, concepts and emotions*

Study tip

Questions relating to why PE is compulsory in school are very popular, with an emphasis on the health issues associated with it.

7.2 National Healthy Schools Programme

The National Healthy Schools Programme was introduced as a long-term initiative designed to make a significant difference to the health and achievement of children and young people. As such, it is closely linked to PE in schools as it shares many of the aims and objectives of the PE curriculum and is complimentary to it. The intention is that through this programme young people will be able to make informed health and life choices in order to reach their full potential, and through this create happier, healthier children who do better in learning and in life.

In order to be successful there is a need for a **whole-school approach** involving working with children and young people, parents, school staff and the whole school community so that these developments and improvements are successfully achieved. The programme is based on a whole-school approach to physical and emotional wellbeing and is focused on four core themes.

1 Personal, social and health education

- Incorporates sex and relationship education and drug education.
- Contributes to the Every Child Matters outcomes for children and young people of being healthy, staying safe, enjoying and achieving, making a positive contribution and **economic wellbeing**.
- Provides children and young people with knowledge, understanding, skills and attitudes to make informed decisions about their lives.

Objectives

Summarise the National Healthy Schools Programme.

Emphasise the necessity of the whole-school approach.

Consider the link it has with the PE curriculum.

Key terms

Whole-school approach: something that is an essential part of everything a school does.

Economic wellbeing: having sufficient income for basic necessities.

A *These children are making the best of the opportunity to enjoy healthy eating*

2 Healthy eating

- Contributes to the Every Child Matters outcomes for children and young people.
- Gives children and young people the confidence, skills, knowledge and understanding to make healthy food choices.
- Healthy and nutritious food and drink are available across the school day.
- The National Healthy Schools Programme and School Food Trust work together to support schools in this area.

3 Physical activity

- Contributes to the Every Child Matters outcomes for children and young people.
- Children and young people are provided with a range of opportunities to be physically active.
- Children understand how physical activity can help them to be more healthy, and how physical activity can improve and be a part of everyday life.

B *These pupils are able to take part in physical activity as it is provided in the PE programme at their school*

4 Emotional health and wellbeing

- Contributes to the five national curriculum outcomes for children and young people.
- Supports vulnerable individuals and groups.
- Establishes a clear bullying policy.
- Establishes behaviour and rewards policies.
- Sets up a confidential pastoral support system for all pupils.

⚯ links

This links to Chapter 4 on diet.

Activity

1 What range of physical activity is provided for in your school and how active are the pupils?

Activity

2 Find out whether your school has National Healthy School status. If it does, check what they had to comply with and if it does not, find out whether or not the school is complying with any of the areas.

Study tip

It will be important to link the four core themes of this programme and to consider it as a whole-school policy, also identifying any direct link it is likely to have in the provision within the PE curriculum.

Extra-curricular provision

For many years extra-curricular activities have traditionally been offered by PE departments and they can be made available in the following ways.

Activity range

It is likely that the school will offer a greater range of extra-curricular activities than they do within the set curriculum as there is no requirement to offer only the traditional sports. Because the opportunities offered are optional and additional staff (other than just the PE specialists) may also be available, there may be a much greater variety of activities made available.

Some of the provision might be more **recreational**, rather than **competitive**, with the focus being on enjoyment for the pleasure of taking part rather than being in an organised team playing against opposition. For this reason membership of a club may be offered, such as fitness training or aerobics, or even membership of societies, such as becoming officials or even supporters, so that alternatives to just participating as a performer can be provided.

Attitudes of staff

Not only the attitudes of the staff, but their interests and abilities will be factors that influence what they propose to offer, in line with their own strengths. Many staff members teach other subjects but are also prepared to help out with the PE department after school in an activity that interests them, such as a martial art. The experience level of the staff is also important as it is more useful if the member of staff has high levels of experience. Attitudes are usually a very positive factor but there could be instances, in some schools, where other staff are not particularly interested in helping out, so this would reduce the range of activities.

Objectives

Consider the range and type of activity that can be offered.

Know what opportunities might be made available to pupils.

Key terms

Recreational: any form of play, amusement or relaxation performed as games, sports or hobbies.

Competitive: an activity that involves some form of contest, rivalry or game.

∞ links

This links to leisure and recreation in Chapter 3 and also to National Curriculum requirements pages 92–93.

A *It might only be possible to offer a martial art such as this as an extra-curricular activity*

Activity

1 Can you find out how many non-PE specialist teachers help out in your school's extra-curricular provision?

Facilities

All schools are either restricted or fortunate with regard to the facilities they may have available. They may be restricted if they do not have the facilities to offer certain activities, such as a pool for swimming. Well-resourced schools may be able to offer a large range of activities with the extra staff they have available but other schools might find that they only have a small number of areas available for the PE department so the programme they can offer will be affected.

Outside visits

One of the most common solutions to a lack of facilities is to arrange visits to other sporting providers, such as ice rinks, ten-pin bowling, climbing walls or even dry ski slopes, so that use can be made of other local facilities.

B   *Visits can be arranged after school for pupils to take part in activities such as ten-pin bowling*

Club links

The extra-curricular time is an excellent opportunity to develop the school/club links and this could include many providers of major games, such as hockey, netball, soccer and basketball, as well as alternative providers such as health clubs or golf clubs.

In this chapter you have learnt:

✔ the ways in which schools provide a PE programme and the programme that they offer

✔ strategies and initiatives that have been introduced and delivered through schools to complement the PE programme

✔ the high-profile health issues and the role the school can play in addressing them.

Revision questions

1 Which of the following terms refers to PE provision that might be provided after school?

a National Curriculum

b Extra-curricular

c Cross-curricular

d Semi-curricular

2 Give three different reasons why PE is offered in schools and explain the benefit to be gained for each one.

3 What is the difference between a foundation subject and a core subject? Which type is PE?

4 Which of the six National Curriculum activity groups would the following subjects be placed in?

a Hockey

b Lifesaving

c Trampoline

d Golf

e Circuit training

f High jumping

g Aerobics

5 How could levels of economic wellbeing affect your personal and social health?

6 What is meant by a 'whole-school approach'?

7 Give four examples of activities you would consider to be mainly recreational ones.

8 How could attitudes of staff affect the amount of extra-curricular provision that a school might be able to provide?

9 In what ways do the facilities a school has shape the extra-curricular provision they are likely to offer?

8 Organisation influences

■ Aims

✔ Be aware of the role of Sport England as a government agency providing funding and facilities, measuring and monitoring participation levels, and identifying specific priority groups.

✔ Be aware of the roles that national governing bodies perform in terms of providing and supporting coaching, assisting with officiating and talent development, and being involved with competition at various levels.

✔ Be aware of the role that the Youth Sport Trust has in managing national school sport competitions and also running leadership and volunteering programmes.

✔ Be aware of the role of the Dame Kelly Holmes Legacy Trust in terms of utilising elite sport role models and assisting in inspiring participation and mentoring young people.

This chapter focuses on some of the organisations that exist to ensure that sport can be provided for all possible participants and that it is run efficiently. Some are linked specifically to the government and some are set up as charities or trusts, but they all receive funding in some form and have to decide how that funding is prioritised and spent. It is important to be aware of the roles that each of them play and to keep up to date with any changes or developments that may occur – that is why you are advised to look at their websites while studying this topic.

All of the organisations are linked to each other, some of them more closely than others, but they all have an underlying aim to increase the opportunities for participation in physical activity.

8.1 Sport England

Sport England is one of the most important organisations that has been set up by the government to help to provide increased opportunities for participation in physical activity.

■ Sport England

Funding

Sport England will invest over £1 billion of National Lottery and **Exchequer** funding between 2012 and 2017 in various organisations and projects, for example:

- Up to 46 of the national governing bodies (NGBs) received £120 million between 2009 and 2013.
- Organisations identified as national partners will receive approximately £10 million.
- Children and young people, through the NGBs and county sports partnerships, received approximately £28 million.
- Open funding makes money available for small grants (£7 million of lottery money), inspired grants (£10 million of lottery money) and protecting playing fields (£3 million of lottery money).
- Mixed funding is based around the legacy of the successful London 2012 Olympics with £30 million available from 2012 to 2015.
- In addition to all of the above, Sport England is also responsible for allocating other National Lottery funding depending on how much is allocated to it by the government. This amount can vary from year to year.

Facilities

Clearly there is a link between facilities and funding as facilities are very expensive to provide, administrate and run.

- Sport England provides a range of facilities and planning services that are linked to helping to plan for good sports facilities to be used now and in the future.
- Help is given to assist in the planning of good facilities.
- There is a specific focus on protecting playing fields as there was a period where many schools and local authorities were selling these to raise money.
- Grants are available to help provide facilities through what is known as the Iconic Facilities Funding, and smaller grants for some other facilities funding are also available.
- Another aim is to improve facility design and concentrate on modernisation of facilities to help to raise standards.

LOTTERY FUNDED

A *The logo for Sport England as the agency that awards funds from the National Lottery*

Key terms

Exchequer: the government department that is in charge of the public revenues, also known as the Treasury.

Ethnic: relating to a group of people with a common national or cultural tradition.

Participation levels

Sport England is committed to carrying out research in order to track the progress of its aim to grow and sustain participation in sport.

■ The Active People Survey measures how many people participate, who they are, what sports they do and how those factors can vary across the different regions of England. This is then reported each year as 'Sport facts' when the results are published in December.

■ There is a specific stated aim of finding out why people play sport, what keeps them engaged and why they drop out.

■ Links have been identified with the effect that economic conditions have on participation in sport and this is connected to the economic recessions that the country has experienced.

B *Sky Ride is a British Cycling initiative that has received Sport England funding. Its aim is to encourage more people to ride bikes*

Priority Groups

Sport England has a commitment to 'helping people and communities across the country create a sporting habit for life'. This includes:

■ creating opportunities for young people to play sport

■ the 'Give sport a go' initiative that links with the NGBs to inform any potential participants about programmes which are running or their nearest clubs.

■ identifying 19 sporting segments for specific consideration (e.g. 'Supportive Single' is the name given to the least active 'segment' who have been identified as likely to be mothers aged between 18 and 25). Other specifically identified groups are the disabled, women and certain **ethnic** groups.

⊙⊙links

This links closely to activity levels and needs on pages 24–25, Chapter 3 on leisure and recreation, Chapter 7 on the role of schools, and Chapter 9 on cultural and social factors.

Activity

Log on to the Sport England website at **www.sportengland. org** to get up-to-date information regarding funding, facilities, participation levels, priority groups and any current developments or initiatives that the organisation has introduced.

Study tip

It is important to be aware of the overall aims of Sport England. You should also know that it was set up by the government and that it is answerable to Parliament through the Department for Culture, Media and Sport.

Questions are often based on the funding role of Sport England, and if you are asked any general funding questions it is important to be aware of the role that Sport England has in this – notably through National Lottery money.

8.2 National governing bodies

The national governing bodies (NGBs) of sport are independent organisations that lead the development and delivery of their sport nationally and locally.

Coaching roles

Each governing body does what it can to provide coaches who are able to supply coaching for their particular sport.

Many NGBs provide specific training at various levels for coaches of their sport. There are usually several levels and coaches can start at a fairly basic point and progress through to higher ones. So a coach could start off working with small groups, often beginners, at a local level and progress right up to working with elite performers at national and international level. The sport of netball is a good example of this as there is what is known as a coaching pathway, which has three levels of coaching awards that are linked to the **United Kingdom Coaching Certificate (UKCC)**.

An organisation called Sports Coach UK was formed as a charity to help to recruit, develop and retain coaches. It currently supports 46 NGBs and 49 county sports partnerships to help them improve their coaching systems, and provides research and good practice that benefits coaching.

Officiating

Each governing body is responsible for setting and interpreting the rules of their particular sport, so this logically links with both training and providing officials.

As well as different levels of coaches, there are also often different levels of officials. Some sports have both minor and major officials who may have very different roles. In football, for instance, there are two assistant referees (who officiate particularly on the sidelines) and the referee, who is in sole charge. In order to become a referee in football, you have to be over 14 years of age and undertake a Basic Referees Course with your local county FA (Football Association, the governing body for football). This then leads on to being a referee at grass-roots level, semi-professional level, up to the Football League, the Premiership and then even to international level. In football it is the responsibility of each level of the game, from county to national, to appoint the referees for their particular games and competitions.

Objectives

Consider the ways in which governing bodies provide and support coaching.

Consider the ways in which governing bodies assist with officiating.

Look at the ways in which governing bodies assist with talent development.

Consider the ways in which governing bodies are involved with competition at various levels.

∞ links

This links with the role of the coach on pages 161–162.

A *Netball has three levels of coaching awards to help netball coaches learn and progress*

∞ links

This links with the role of the official on page 162.

Talent development

Each particular sport wants their sport to be successful and also to develop. This can only be achieved if they are able to keep up standards.

An individual who has a particular **talent** for a sport first has to be spotted and then their skills have to be developed. An organisation known as UK Sport has formed the UK Talent Team to support sports so that they can improve their systems of performance. It has run seven national athlete recruitment projects that have assessed more than 7,000 new performers who were previously unknown. As a result of these projects, 100 athletes were selected for the World Class system. They have made 293 international appearances and won a total of 102 international medals.

Once a talented performer has been identified and linked to the NGB, the coaching, support (and often funding) is provided to enable the individual to develop to their full potential.

Competition

One of the main aims of any NGB is to provide competition for the individuals who participate in their sport.

Competitions are normally arranged at all levels of the sport. They can be regional, district, county, national and international. In some sports there may be individual or team competitions and many sports have a combination of both.

One of the main reasons for competitions to be arranged at different levels is so that competitors can progress to the varying standards. The competitions get harder as they advance towards the highest level. NGBs often use competitions to enable them to select teams and competitors to represent their sport at national and international levels.

B *Competitors at the England Athletics National Championships, which is used in selecting the national team*

Key terms

United Kingdom Coaching Certificate (UKCC): a government-led initiative that is an endorsement of a sport-specific coach education programme.

Talent: a special natural ability or aptitude.

Activity

1 Look at the websites for UK Sport (**www.uksport. gov.uk**) and Sports Coach UK (**www.sportscoachuk. org**) to find out about any new or recent developments that these organisations have been involved in.

2 Choose a particular sport that you are interested in and find out who the governing body is. Look at their website to see what support they provide.

∞links

This links to competitions on pages 130–131.

Study tip

All NGBs have responsibility for the factors identified in this unit, but it is a good idea to choose one particular body that you are specifically interested in and find out how they deal with all of the aspects identified.

If a specific question is asked, you will then be able to give actual examples relating to a particular sport and the ways in which the NGB achieves its aims.

8.3 Youth Sport Trust

The Youth Sport Trust is an independent charity devoted to changing young people's lives through sport. Its aim is to achieve this through high-quality physical education and sport opportunities.

■ Managing competitions

Every year the Youth Sport Trust runs several events including camps, national conferences and national school sport events.

The first National School Games (also known as the Sainsbury's School Games as they are sponsored by Sainsbury's supermarket chain) were held in 2012 at the Olympic Park. These games took over from the previous UK School Games, which ran from 2006 to 2011. This is a multi-sport event that more than 1,500 young people compete in. Competition takes place in 12 current and future Olympic and Paralympic sports: fencing, rugby sevens, gymnastics, hockey, badminton, athletics, cycling, judo, swimming, table tennis, volleyball and wheelchair basketball. This event usually takes place over three days and more than 700 coaches, support staff and volunteers help to organise and run the event. The Youth Sport Trust is responsible for developing and organising the Games. There is a considerable amount of organisation involved as the events, such as those based in Sheffield in 2013, use several different venues to accommodate the various sports.

There are four levels in the Sainsbury's School Games involving competition in schools, between schools, at county/area level leading up to the national finals event. The four levels that are established are:

- Level 1 – sporting competition for all students in school through intra-school competition
- Level 2 – individuals and teams are selected to represent their schools in local inter-school competitions
- Level 3 – the county/area stages multi-sport Sainsbury's School Games festivals as a culmination of year-round school sport competition
- Level 4 – the Sainsbury's School Games, which then becomes the final event and competition.

Objectives

Consider the ways in which the Youth Sport Trust manages national school sport competitions.

Look at the ways in which the Youth Sport Trust provides and manages leadership and volunteering programmes.

Activity

Organisations such as the Youth Sport Trust are very dependent upon government funding, and this funding can change at short notice. New initiatives can also be introduced. Therefore, it is important to keep up to date with developments by looking at the Trust's website **www. youthsporttrust.org**.

A *Young people attending the first Sainsbury's School Games held at the Olympic Park in 2012*

Leadership and volunteering programmes

The main aim of these programmes is to engage young people in PE and school sport.

Following the successful 2012 London Olympics, a **legacy commitment** was made to ensure that young people were at the heart of the initiative. The Lead Your Generation initiative was started by the Youth Sport Trust to help to empower young people to be **role models** and make a difference in their school and community. This is achieved through the young people working collaboratively with teachers, as a cluster of schools and with community groups to develop legacy action plans for their schools and local communities.

The Lead Your Generation initiative links to the Young Ambassadors movement, which was established prior to the 2012 Games when over 5000 young people were involved. They were selected as being the most outstanding sports leaders in schools due to their sporting talent, exceptional commitment and ability as young leaders or volunteers. The Young Ambassadors have specific roles and they aim to increase participation and healthy lifestyles within their school, promote the positive values of sport in and through sport, be role models in advocating PE and school sport, and be the young people's voice on PE and school sport in their schools and communities. There are four categories of Young Ambassadors, starting with primary-aged children who are Bronze Young Ambassadors, Silver Young Ambassadors (who work within their own school), Gold Young Ambassadors (who work across a local area and are trained specifically by the Youth Sport Trust) and Platinum Young Ambassadors (who have spent at least a year as a Gold Young Ambassador).

Sport relies on over 1.5 million volunteers, officials, coaches, administrators and managers. The Youth Sport Trust has started the SISVP (Step into Sport Volunteer Passport) to provide young people with the opportunity to log and record their volunteering hours and experiences and be rewarded and recognised for this. These young people are recognised as being the future sporting workforce who can be developed and deployed in meaningful volunteering roles.

Key terms

Legacy commitment: a plan to harness the enthusiasm generated by the London 2012 Olympics and to ensure that it continues.

Role models: people who others might aspire to be like, they are looked up to and seen as good examples.

∞ links

There are clear links here to role models on pages 142–143.

∞ links

There are clear links here with school and physical education, covered in Chapter 7.

Study tip

It is important to be aware of the precise role that the Youth Sport Trust plays with regard to managing competitions, leadership and volunteering rather than many of the other roles that they also undertake.

Questions asked are likely to focus on the way in which the work that the organisation does can help to increase participation, and how the Trust achieves its aim of engaging young people in PE and school sport.

B *Young Ambassadors who have been developed as volunteers by the Youth Sport Trust*

8.4 The Dame Kelly Holmes Legacy Trust

Kelly Holmes was the first British female to win both the 800 metres and the 1500 metres in the 2004 Olympic Games, and she was appointed a Dame in 2005. The Dame Kelly Holmes Legacy Trust was started in 2008.

Elite sport role models

A large group of top sports performers known as 'champions' work with young people to help to inspire them and help them to learn from the experience of world-class sports stars.

- Since 2008 the Dame Kelly Holmes Legacy Trust has helped over 100 world-class athletes to further their careers. This is achieved by giving them access to appropriate support and development opportunities, and by providing a high-quality career transition programme, **bespoke** professional development support and routes into sport and education, and high-quality work placements and employment opportunities.

- The National Support Programme was set up for elite sports performers who are in the process of transitioning from international competition to new careers. A sports performer's competitive career can be relatively short, so it is important that they are able to plan for the future and take on different roles. The Trust has a Champions Zone that provides advice regarding a range of different employment development opportunities. Many champions of the past who have moved on to other careers are on hand to give advice and support after they have attended a 'Next Steps' session.

- The BOA Athlete Career Programme provides placement support that in turn helps to provide skills and training.

- An Elite Coaching Team is also available, and this team has business and support experience in order to help with personal and professional development.

Objectives

Look at the ways in which the Dame Kelly Holmes Legacy Trust utilises elite sport role models.

Consider the ways in which the Trust assists in inspiring participation and mentoring young people.

Key terms

Bespoke: designed for a particular individual.

Mentors: influential, trusted and experienced advisers.

∞ **links**

This links to role models on pages 142–143.

A Dame Kelly Holmes with her Olympic gold medals

Young people

The Trust's aim is 'getting young lives on track' and this is achieved by offering support for young people.

- Central to this aim is the belief that all young people need a hero who they can look up to and be inspired by and who is able to help them make the best of their talents and abilities. The sporting role models who are linked to the trust are therefore used to raise the aspirations of young people.
- The elite athletes act as **mentors** to young people on the charity projects that the Trust runs.

Projects

The Trust runs a range of charity projects in order to achieve its aims, including:

- *Get on Track* – this provides disadvantaged young people with the chance to enhance their confidence, self-belief and employability skills.
- *AQA Unlocking Potential* – working with AQA (the exam board for this GCSE), 20 young people are selected to take part in a combination of personal development challenges and social action projects.
- *National Citizen Service* – this is another personal development programme run by the government's Big Society scheme helping young people to prepare for adult life.
- *Sport for Change* – this project helps young homeless people through a six-week personal development programme.
- *Aspiring Minds* – this is a school-based programme designed to develop the skills and attitudes required for success in the modern world.
- *Sporting Champions* – this initiative is a Sport England one and the Trust uses the role-model programme in partnership with Creating Excellence.
- *Young People Re-engagement Programme* – the Trust works with two other partners (Skill Force and By Design) to help young people who are at risk of exclusion from mainstream education.

B *Dame Kelly Holmes with a young person from the charity's Get on Track programme*

Activity

As with other organisations, the Dame Kelly Holmes Legacy Trust is likely to set up new initiatives and new charity projects, so you should access the website **www. dkhlegacytrust.org** to keep up with changes and developments.

⚭ links

This links to cultural and social factors in Chapter 9.

Study tip

It is likely that a question could be asked about how elite performers are used to mentor young people and the effect that this mentoring has. To help you with this, it would be a good idea to look at one of the case studies that are available on the Trust's website.

kerboodle

8

In this chapter you have learnt:

✔ how Sport England funds sport and sporting organisations and assists in providing facilities as well as measuring levels of participation and identifying priority groups

✔ the roles that the different national governing bodies carry out for their particular sports in providing and supporting coaching, helping with officiating and talent development, and also being involved with competition at various levels

✔ the role of the Youth Sport Trust in managing the national school sport competitions and running leadership and volunteering programmes

✔ how the Dame Kelly Holmes Legacy Trust utilises elite sport role models and helps to inspire the participation and mentoring of young people.

Revision questions

1 Which of the following is not a role that a national governing body would carry out?

a Setting rules

b Training and providing officials

c Support coaching

d Organising the national school sports competitions

2 What is the main source of income that Sport England receives and in what way does it distribute that funding?

3 How does Sport England go about helping to raise levels of participation in sport?

4 How do national governing bodies go about providing and supporting coaching in particular sports?

5 What types of competition do national governing bodies get involved in organising?

6 Which particular major competition is the Youth Sport Trust specifically involved in?

7 In what ways does the Youth Sport Trust set up and administer leadership and volunteering programmes?

8 How does the Dame Kelly Holmes Legacy Trust make use of elite sport role models?

9 Name a project that has been set up by the Dame Kelly Holmes Legacy Trust and describe what it sets out to do.

9 Cultural and social factors

Aims

✔ Understand the concept of leisure time and what might be available.

✔ Be aware of different types of user groups.

✔ Understand the concept of fair play and correct etiquette and give examples of these.

✔ Be aware of different types of social groupings and understand the positive and negative effects these groups can have on an individual.

This chapter focuses on influential factors that are likely to affect levels of participation among individuals. They include factors that the individual may not have any control over, such as gender or ethnicity, and those where some form of choice is available regarding possible outcomes, such as family and peer pressure.

This is part of the overall key influences, which in turn leads to making informed decisions about getting involved in a lifetime of healthy physical activities. Where social groupings may impose some restrictions, the social aspects section looks at the types of opportunities that might be available and where the element of choice exists.

9.1 Social aspects

The following factors can affect the type and level of participation in physical activity.

■ Leisure time

This the time that you have at your disposal and that is free for you to decide what you do with it. This is therefore the time that you are not at school or work, so it mainly consists of evenings and weekends. The opportunities available for leisure time have increased in recent years for the following reasons:

- *Higher levels of unemployment* – people who are not able to obtain full-time work have the majority of their time available to them.

- *A shorter working week* – for many people this means that they will finish work earlier and have more opportunities either during a specific day or late afternoon/early evening.

- *Part-time and shift work* – means that at any time during the day some people have available leisure time.

- *Technological advances* – such as labour saving devices (washing machines, etc.) can release some time. The growth of the internet means that many workers are able to work from home, so the time previously taken up by travelling could become leisure time.

Because of this trend for more leisure time, there becomes a necessity for providers to be available who can cater for those people who want to make active use of it. Many local authorities (the organisations who manage and run leisure centres) and also private clubs who make up

A *These mothers are able to take part in an organised class while their children are being cared for*

Objectives

Understand the concept of leisure time and look at the types of provisions that can be made for it.

Be aware of specifically identifiable user groups.

Understand the concepts of fair play and correct etiquette.

∞ links

There is a considerable link to leisure and recreation in Chapter 3.

the **leisure industry** have grown in direct response to the increased need. They have identified some particular **user groups** and have targeted their provision specifically at them. Examples of these include:

- mothers and toddlers
- unemployed people
- shift workers.

Fairness and personal and social responsibility

Anyone taking part in any form of organised sport is expected to do so in the correct way and this includes making sure that they understand the concept of **etiquette**. Some examples of this include:

- kicking the ball out of play to enable a referee to stop the game for an injured player to receive treatment
- shaking hands with opponents before and after any game.

B *This match has been deliberately stopped by a player kicking the ball out of play in order to allow the referee to stop the game, allowing the injured Alexander Hleb to be treated*

Participants should also ensure that they understand the role that rules play in order to make an activity fair. This can include:

- playing in the spirit of the game and not trying to 'bend' the rules to an unfair advantage
- responding positively to the officials in charge (including teachers) and treating them with respect
- playing fairly to ensure that you are playing safely.

Activity

1 Find out which 'user groups' your local leisure centre specifically caters for.

Key terms

Leisure industry: any provider that provides opportunities for people in their available leisure time.

User groups: particular groups of people who use leisure facilities.

Etiquette: the unwritten rules or conventions of any activity.

Activity

2 Find out what constitutes the 'leisure industry' in your particular area. Make a note of the different options available to anyone to make use of their leisure time.

links

Fair play links closely to health and safety and sport and equipment rules on pages 144–147.

Study tip

You should be able to define correct etiquette and be able to give an example from a sporting situation. You can use examples from you own experience or from watching sporting events.

9.2 Social groupings

Any form of social group is likely to influence your level and type of participation in any activity and it can be a major influence on physical activity.

Peers

When you are in your teens and in school your **peer group** is one of the greatest influences upon you and can have both positive and negative effects.

- If your peers are actively involved in sport and physical activities, this is likely to have a positive effect, as you will want to join in with them.
- If your peer group are not in favour of regular physical activity, choose alternative leisure and recreation activities, or have a negative view of PE lessons, it is likely that you will go along with these views too.

Peer-group pressure can be very difficult to resist and many young people find that this shapes their attitudes and behaviour throughout their school lives.

Family

This is clearly another group that has a tremendous amount of influence upon a young person and there may be both positive and negative influences here too.

- Positive effects could be the level of support they may be willing to give. This could be financial through providing specialist equipment, kit or even payment for coaching and development. It could also involve providing transport for training or competing, or just as simple as watching and supporting when you are taking part. Many parents are also role models as their children might want to follow in a sporting tradition set by them.

> **Objectives**
>
> Be aware of the different types of social groupings that exist.
>
> Understand the influences and effects these groups can have, both positively and negatively.

∞ links

See the sections on leisure and recreation in Chapter 3.

∞ links

See the section on role models on pages 142–143.

A *Parents and family supporting their children when they take part can greatly encourage them to be involved in sport and PE*

- Negative effects can be the reverse of all of the above when family members are either not prepared or not able to provide the support. Some family members may have had a negative experience that has put them off physical activity, there may be concerns over safety or even pressure to concentrate on academic work rather than practical physical activity.

Gender

This is far less of an issue that it used to be as there are now more opportunities for women to access as many sports as men do, and more women are becoming officials and obtaining management roles.

B   *Joan Benoit winning the first Olympic women's marathon, at the 1984 Los Angeles Olympics. Previously women were not thought to be capable enough to be able to run it!*

Ethnicity

Ethnic background can be a factor especially in a culture where women are not encouraged to take part in PE on religious grounds owing to constraints on what they might be required to wear.

Key terms

Peer group: people of the same age and status as you.

Peer-group pressure: where the peer group will attempt to persuade an individual to follow their lead.

Ethnic: a group of people with a common national or cultural tradition.

Activity

Find out about other women's events or activities that were only recently introduced to major competitions. Start with the pole vault and long jump events.

Study tip

For all of the above social groupings, you are likely to be asked for the positive and negative effects they may have. Try not to just consider opposites but come up with different examples for both types of effect.

9

In this chapter you have learnt:

✔ what leisure time is and how the leisure industry has grown to cater for it

✔ the different types of user groups that can be identified and the ways in which they can be catered for

✔ why playing fairly is important and desirable

✔ what is meant by correct etiquette and examples where this can be shown

✔ what the different types of social groupings are

✔ the influence that these social groupings can have on an individual.

Revision questions

1 Which of the following is not an example of a user group?
  a Mothers and toddlers
  b Senior citizens
  c Shift workers
  d A first-aid group

2 Why has the leisure industry grown in recent years?

3 What is actually meant by a person's leisure time?

4 What is meant by the term 'etiquette'?

5 Choose three different physical activities and give a different example of correct etiquette that you would associate with that activity.

6 What is the link between fair play and safety?

7 What is meant by the term 'peer pressure'?

8 Using a different example for each, explain the effect your peers might have on your level of participation in:
  a a positive way
  b a negative way.

9 How might your family have a positive effect upon your participation in physical activities?

10 In what ways have women been discriminated upon in the past in terms of participating in physical activity?

11 What cultural and ethnic factors might affect the levels of participation in physical activity?

Aims

✔ Understand the different roles you may be able to adopt.

✔ Be aware of the available career and vocation opportunities.

✔ Be aware of additional qualifications you may be able to study for and obtain.

✔ Be aware of links of PE with other school subjects.

This chapter focuses on the ways you can develop your interest and study of PE, as well as the opportunities and pathways that might enable you to become or remain involved in physical activities.

You may have to take on different roles as part of your course, on which you will be assessed and marked. It is possible to take on more than one of these, rather than only as a performer. If you are taking the Double Award you might need to look at the different roles that are available to you, some of which can lead on to career opportunities as well.

Your GCSE in PE is likely to be the first step on your way to obtaining nationally recognised qualifications, as you will be able to see the range of different qualifications available to you as you carry on with your academic career, perhaps even to university level. Not all career paths need academic qualifications, however, and you are also able to get specific awards and coaching certificates through the national governing bodies (NGBs).

Finally, make use of the cross-curricular links identified – you might be surprised how much of the work that you need to learn and know will also be covered elsewhere in school.

10.1 Physical activity roles

One of the most important aspects of this examination is that individuals can participate in different ways. It is not just restricted to being an actual performer but can be any way that enables you to be an active participant. The following is a basic overview of the different roles that may be chosen.

Player/performer

This is primarily concerned with developing the ability to make effective plans to improve performance. If you are taking part in a games activity, then you will be a player but you will be a performer if you are taking part in gymnastics or dance, for example.

In order to be able to bring about improvements in your performance you need to ensure that you have a good knowledge of the particular activity and of the skills, **tactics**, playing positions, **techniques** and moves that are essential for that particular activity.

Organiser

This role involves bringing together all the main ingredients at the right time, in the right place, in order to maximise promotion, participation and high-quality performance.

An organiser will have to be competent in managing and organising available facilities, time, personnel and even funds at times. They will also be working at different levels and undertake quite a large range of duties and responsibilities.

Leader/coach

This is a specialist in an activity, responsible for preparing a player in skill acquisition, correct technique, physical or mental state. Leaders/coaches are important in influencing individuals or groups to achieve set goals or in behaviour in sport. It is important for them to know about particular styles of leadership that might be used, as well as to have some good basic communication skills.

Choreographer

This involves being the designer or arranger of some sort of staged dance, ballet or other performance and applies specifically to exploring and communicating ideas, concepts and emotions, for example in dance activities. They would need to be aware of the techniques of choreography and to be able to assess levels or standards of performance.

Objectives

Be aware of the different roles that can be adopted.

Develop knowledge and understanding of what each role constitutes.

Consider appropriate roles you might be able to adopt.

Key terms

Tactics: pre-arranged and rehearsed strategies or methods of play.

Technique: the manner or way in which someone carries out or performs a particular skill.

∞ links

All of the roles of an active participant are dealt with in greater detail in Chapter 13, where there is a more detailed breakdown of the options and responsibilities that each role encompasses.

Activity

1 Make a decision about a role you would like to adopt, other than that of performer. You are going to have to be assessed on this at least once, so you should start to consider it as soon as possible. Observing or even talking to someone already adopting that role would be very useful.

A choreographer's role involves directing how a performance should be presented

Official

This is someone who controls the activity, interprets the rules, laws or regulations of the activity, and checks equipment. There are different possibilities within this role, such as:

- referee/umpire
- judge.

There are many qualities required in order to be an official, but it is vital that you know the rules or regulations of the activity you are going to be involved in.

B *Taking on the role of an official could include refereeing a match*

10.2 Vocational opportunities

Part of the reason for taking a GCSE course in PE may well be to prepare yourself for some particular career or job in the future and there are various **vocations** that you might consider.

Sports performers

There are increasingly more opportunities to become a performer, with three basic categories available.

Professional

This is someone who takes part in a sport or an activity for their livelihood. They will get paid for taking part and will do it as a full-time job.

Amateur

This is someone who takes part in a sport or activity as a pastime or hobby rather than for any financial gain. They take part for the enjoyment factor, do not get paid and usually also have a job. In some activities it is actually forbidden for an amateur to receive any money at all.

Semi-professional

This is a combination of both of the above as it is someone who might have a job but who also takes part in sport for payment. They would usually work full-time and play sport in their spare time, but some also work part-time so that they can train and play over a longer period.

Not all sport is quite as straightforward as this. Some sports are **open sports**, in many amateur sports there are various loopholes that enable the amateur players to receive money, and there are even **shamateurs** in many sports as well! Some of these loopholes include:

- *Sponsorship deals* – the performer is given equipment, clothing, training facilities, free travel and even cash payments in return for endorsing a particular make or product.
- *Occupations* – a 'job' that includes a great deal of time off to train and compete.
- *Expenses payments* – these are often far more than the expenses actually incurred and are effectively just cash payments.
- *Scholarships* – universities and colleges offer sports scholarships, which then allow full-time sport to be carried out.

Activity

1 Find out about sports and activities that are 'open sport' and also any that are completely amateur.

Objectives

Consider the type, variety and extent of vocations that might be available.

Consider the differences between amateur and professional sport.

Be aware of the particular careers that might be accessible.

A *Ernie Els victorious with Claret Jug trophy after winning the British Open, an example of an open sport competition where amateurs and professionals compete together*

⚭ links

See pages 138–141 for further information about the role of sponsors and the influence of sponsorship and also how these may link to physical activity roles on pages 116–117.

Activity

2   See whether you can find out about any specific sports scholarships that are made available – many US universities offer them.

Careers

There are now many career opportunities available in what is becoming known as the 'sport and leisure industry' and they include the following:

- PE teacher
- Coach
- Trainer
- Physiotherapist
- Sports management
- Personal trainer.

These are just a few examples of the vocational opportunities currently available and the different positions that are being developed and made available.

Key terms

Vocation: a regular occupation for which you would be particularly qualified or suited.

Open sport: an activity that allows both amateurs and professionals to compete together.

Shamateur: someone who competes in an amateur sport but who receives illegal payments.

Study tip

The difference between amateur and professional sport is a popular topic to be questioned on, as well as the ways in which amateurs are able to get around the rules relating to their status.

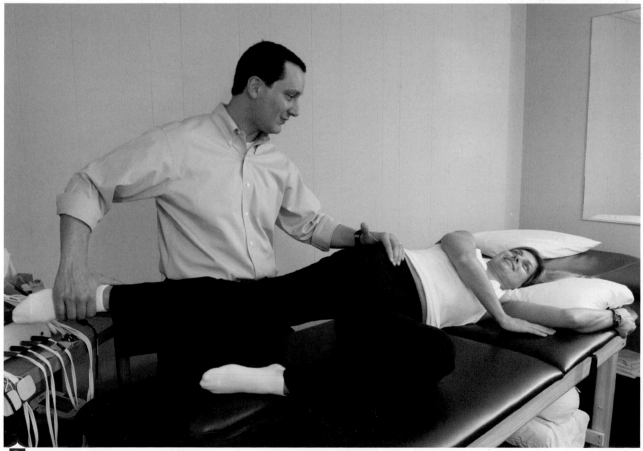

B   *A career in physiotherapy could be a particular vocation linked to following a PE course*

10.3 Further qualifications

There are now a great many **accredited** courses and qualifications that are available relating to PE and sport.

BTEC

These qualifications were introduced as recently as 2002. They are diplomas in sport, equivalent to GCSEs and vocationally based, with a basic grounding in understanding and knowledge of the sports sector.

GCSE

This includes the course you are currently studying and it is possible to make this a Double Award worth two GCSEs. As well as GCSE PE, there is also a separate GCSE in dance. GCSEs are an important first step towards higher-level qualifications, but it is quite important to achieve higher grade passes (from grade C upwards) in order to go on to the next level of qualification.

GCE

These are the next level of exam qualification up from GCSEs and are divided into two parts: the AS level, taken in the first year, and then the A2 in the following year, in order to achieve the full A Level, which is graded in the same way as the GCSE. A points system related to the grades achieved is the way that university places are decided upon and it is possible to continue with a PE qualification up to A Level standard.

Sports performance awards

There are an increasing number of these awards that are becoming available, many linked to specific sports, such as athletics. Another type that is often offered in schools is the Sports Leaders UK Level 1 Award in Sports Leadership, which is open to anyone aged 14 and older. This award can lead on to further qualifications, such as the Level 2 Award in Community Sports Leadership for young people over 16, and there are a great deal more awards available beyond this.

Objectives

Outline some of the types and varieties of accredited courses.

Consider some of the career pathways these qualifications may lead to.

Key terms

Accredited: a recognised standard of award leading on to a higher learning level.

Proficiency: being adequately or well qualified.

∞ links

For more details about Sports Leaders UK Awards visit **www.sportsleaders.org**, which lists all the courses available.

A *Successfully studying for your GCSE in PE could well be the first step towards further study and a specific career*

Proficiency testing and awards

Owing to the number of sports and activities, an increasing number of **proficiency** awards are being made available. These are often developed and made available through the NGBs (national governing bodies) and many of them are delivered by schools. Many PE departments use award schemes to test and reward activities, such as gymnastics and athletics, and many swimming awards can qualify people for personal survival or as lifesavers. If you wanted to get a job as a lifesaver in a local swimming pool you would have to have an up-to-date lifesaving award.

Activities

1. Carry out a survey of the number of proficiency awards that might be available within your school or partner schools. Find out at least three NGB awards that are currently available.

2. Find out detailed information about one of the further qualifications that interests you most and see what is required to study for it.

∞ links

Awards may well be directly linked to vocational opportunities as outlined on pages 118–119.

Study tip

While you will not be tested on exactly what a specific award is, you might well be asked what the benefits would be of following an examination course. You will be able to use your own experiences as examples here.

B *All pool lifeguards have to have a current, updated lifesaving qualification in order to perform their role*

10.4 / Cross-curricular links

Most subjects link in some way to others and PE makes many links across other areas of the curriculum.

English

The skills of speaking and listening are clearly very important, but in PE one of the most important links with English is making use of the specialised vocabulary that is needed. Many words have very specific meanings within PE, 'power' for example. In PE terms it would be referred to as the combination of strength and speed, as opposed to other dictionary definitions.

Another clear link with English is the ability to be able to write clearly, in an examination answer for example!

Mathematics

Quite a lot of practical maths is included in PE, such as measuring and recording in athletics, estimating distances, and using basic mathematical skills to fill in scorebooks in cricket and basketball. Some quite complex maths problems could be posed for a captain in cricket, who may need to keep account of overs left to be bowled, run rates and deliveries left. Most darts players are excellent at very quick mental arithmetic!

⊂⊃ **links**

Chapters 2 and 5 have many science aspects within them.

Science

The GCSE specification has firmly identified links with science (single and double award) – biology, human biology and human physiology and health. At least eight of the specific areas covered in this examination are also covered in some of the above!

Geography

The most obvious link here is with orienteering, where there is a need to be able to read maps and understand specific symbols. However, any outdoor pursuit participant needs to know about landscapes, weather patterns and even specific geographical features, which are particularly important to climbers and cavers.

Food technology

All of the basic information about diet and nutrition is essential and knowledge of the balance of energy intake through the nutrients in food is essential for all sports performers. Some performers will need specific diets so they will need to know the specific food groups to include.

A *You need a lot of geographical skills to be able to take part in orienteering successfully*

B *Learning about a balanced diet is something that might be taught in Food Technology*

Citizenship

This may be a subject taught specifically in some schools, but many schools try to include it in the delivery of other subjects, such as PE. The themes and values of trust, responsibility, **inclusion**, **equity** and respect are all core themes, which it is widely recognised can be taught through taking part in games.

> ### Activity
>
> See how many of the core citizenship themes you can identify that you might have covered in some way in your PE programme – especially a game activity!

Music

There is an obvious link here with dance specifically, and even aerobics, where music is likely to be used as a stimulus to a performance and knowledge of composition and rhythm is important.

PHSE

This is also often taught as a specific subject and the areas of developing relationships based on trust and honesty, learning to cope with success and failure, taking criticism and acting on it and developing awareness of strengths and weaknesses can all be linked to PE.

∞ links

There is a very specific link here with diet in Chapter 4.

> ### Key terms
>
> **Inclusion:** a policy that no one should experience barriers to learning as a result of their disability, heritage, gender, special educational need, ethnicity, social group, sexual orientation, race or culture.
>
> **Equity:** something that is fair, just and impartial.

> ### Study tip
>
> You are unlikely to be asked a question specifically about a link with another particular subject, but you will need to know how PE can contribute to other subjects and where they link in to PE.

Chapter summary

10

In this chapter you have learnt:

✓ what the different roles are that you may choose to adopt with a brief overview of what they involve

✓ the types of vocational opportunities that might be available for you to consider, not only during your course but afterwards

✓ which qualifications you could consider taking in the future to build upon the work and study you will have undertaken for this course

✓ about the many different links that PE has with other subjects taught in the curriculum and the benefits of covering some of the topics in those subjects as well.

Revision questions

1 Which of the following would not be an acceptable role for you to adopt in your PE course?
   a Performer
   b First aider
   c Coach
   d Choreographer

2 What do you think are the most important qualities that an organiser needs to have?

3 Describe three important qualities that an official will need to have in order to be most effective.

4 What is meant by the term 'vocation'?

5 What is the main difference between a professional sportsperson and an amateur?

6 What is a semi-professional sportsperson? Give an example of an activity where these are common.

7 Describe three ways in which an amateur may try to get around some of the rules that particularly apply to them.

8 What is meant by the term 'open sport'? Give at least two examples of this.

9 For an activity of your choice, describe any particular award scheme that is associated with it and name the governing body that administers it.

10 What is meant by the term 'inclusion' in regard to PE and the school curriculum?

11 Choose two subjects, other than PE, and describe the specific links they have with your GCSE PE course.

■ Aims

✔ Be aware of some of the major international sporting events.

✔ Consider other high-profile events.

✔ Understand the importance of the Olympic Games as an international event.

✔ Consider the advantages and disadvantages of hosting major events.

✔ Be aware of the different types and levels of competitions that can be used together and know the advantages and disadvantages of each.

This chapter looks at the impact and importance that sport has as an international factor and as something that has a high profile throughout the world.

International sporting events are now very important throughout the world and covered extensively in the media, with a constant provision of events, contests and competitions in any number of sporting activities. Each major sport has its own competitions, including lesser known sports, and they often reach their peak in the year when the Olympic Games take place, held over a four-week period. The competition to become hosts for the Olympic Games and other major competitions is fierce as the benefits to be gained by the host nation or city are considerable.

Within the Olympic Games, and in all forms of sport, there is an element of competition and many other competitions have become major events in their own right. However, at no matter what level sport is played, there is always organised competition, with different formats used and promoted. All are designed to result in the maximum amount of tension and excitement in the major final.

International sport is now very big business and headline news in the media – not always for the right reasons!

11.1 International sporting events

International sport has grown to be extremely popular among competitors as it is the ultimate aim of everyone to compete at this level. It is also very popular with those who run the events as it is usually very successful and profitable. The following are examples of these types of high-profile events.

◼ World championships

The majority of sports provide a world championship for their particular event.

Football

The World Cup first started in 1930 and has been held every four years since then, except in 1942 and 1946 due to the Second World War. It is the most widely viewed sporting event in the world – an estimated billion people watched the 2010 FIFA World Cup in South Africa.

Rugby

The Rugby World Cup was first held in 1987 and the trophy awarded is known as the William Webb Ellis Cup, named after the person credited with inventing the game. This competition is also held every four years,.

Cricket

This is competed for as a one-day event (as opposed to five-day **test matches**) and was first started in 1975, with entry restricted to the 10 test-playing and one-day international-playing nations and those nations who gain entry through a qualifying competition. It is held every four years.

A *Spain proudly show off the FIFA World Cup Trophy in 2010*

Athletics

This was only started as a world championship comparatively recently, in 1991. It was originally held every four years, but it is now held every two years, on either side of the Olympic Games.

Formula One

The first world championship for Formula One racing was held in 1950 and it has grown to be one of the most popular annual events, televised around the world.

Objectives

Outline the major international sporting events.

Consider some of the other high-profile events.

∞ links

The Olympic Games is also an extremely high-profile event, but it is dealt with separately on pages 128–129.

Activity

1. Find out about world championships or world cups that are organised in other activities. Also find out about any sports or activities that have world championships specifically for women.

High-profile events

Not all sports or activities have their own world championships, but they still remain very popular in the **media**.

- *Wimbledon* – there is no organised world championship for tennis, but this tournament has been in existence since 1877 and is one of the most famous events.

B *Serena Williams competing at Wimbledon. Wimbledon is still considered by many to be the most important tennis tournament to win.*

- *Super Bowl* – this is the most watched US television broadcast of the year and also has a very large world audience.
- *Football leagues* – leagues, such as the Premiership and Champions League, are very popular and attract very large audiences, sponsorship and financial backing.
- *One-off events* – these sporting contests, such as some boxing events, are very popular and regularly arranged and promoted.

The above are just examples of what is available in terms of international sport, concentrating on the most famous and popular ones, but there are international sporting competitions and events in all sports.

Key terms

Test match: a match played in cricket or rugby by all-star teams from different countries.

Media: the various forms of mass communication, such as radio, TV and the press.

Activity

2 Find out what the most popular international sporting event is. Look at actual attendance figures as well as viewing figures.

⚭ links

For the links between the role and influence of the media and of sponsors and sponsorship in international sport, see pages 134–141. There are also links with competitions on pages 130–131.

Study tip

You will not be asked about any specific event or competition but you might well be tested on what makes something high profile and to explain why it is so popular.

11.2 The Olympic Games

History of the Olympic Games

The Olympic Games is probably the highest-profile sporting event that takes place and an important event in its own right. It was first held in 776 BC in Olympia, Greece. The International Olympic Committee (IOC) was founded in 1894 and the first IOC Summer Olympic Games was held in 1896 in Athens. The games are held every four years, throughout the world, after a complicated and lengthy procedure to select the hosts.

In recent years there has been much controversy associated with the event, which has created some of the problems outlined below.

Berlin 1936

Adolph Hitler ruled Germany at the head of his Nazi Party, using the Games for **propaganda** purposes to promote his racist views about Jewish and black people. The black American athlete, Jesse Owens, won four gold medals to Hitler's obvious disapproval.

Munich 1972

These Games were marred by a terrorist attack on the Israeli team in the Olympic Village, staged by Palestinian terrorists. Eleven hostages, five terrorists and a police officer were killed as the siege was televised throughout the world. Security issues have dominated ever since.

Montreal 1976

South Africa was banned from taking part due to its **apartheid** policy. There was a **boycott** by many African countries and some others, with 30 nations refusing to send teams in total because the IOC refused to ban New Zealand, whose rugby team had been touring South Africa. The financial cost of staging the Games meant that Montreal was still paying off the debt over 30 years later!

Moscow 1980

The Soviet Union (Russia) invaded Afghanistan in late 1979, so the USA refused to send its team in protest and Great Britain advised competitors not to go. In the end, a total of 52 nations boycotted these Games, which reduced the standard of the competition.

Los Angeles 1984

The Games had already been awarded to this US city some time before, so in retaliation (the excuse was concerns over security) the Soviet Union, together with 14 other nations, boycotted the Games! This was the first Olympic Games to make a profit (officially a 'surplus') owing to the advantage that was taken of the commercial opportunities, which made other countries more interested in being hosts in the future.

Because the Olympic Games has such a high profile, it seems to attract bad publicity regarding security issues, drug taking, boycotts, protests, corruption and claims of over-commercialism.

Objectives

Outline the importance of the Olympic Games as an international event.

Outline some controversy associated with the event.

Consider the advantages and disadvantages of hosting such an event.

A *Jesse Owens competing in the 1936 Berlin Olympic Games, where he won four gold medals*

∞ links

This is closely linked to issues surrounding the role and influence of the media and of sponsorship outlined on pages 134–141, as well as international sporting events on pages 126–127.

Key terms

Propaganda: messages aimed at influencing the behaviour or opinions of large numbers of people.

Apartheid: a policy of separating groups, especially because of race or colour.

Boycott: not using or dealing with something, as a protest.

B *The lighting of the torch at the opening ceremony of the 2012 London Olympics*

◼ Hosting the Games

There is never a shortage of volunteers to host the Olympics, or other major international events, as the advantages are seen to outweigh the disadvantages.

Advantages

- The likelihood of making a profit through sponsorship, media rights and marketing/merchandise.
- The provision of updated or new facilities that can be used again later.
- Raising the profile and reputation of the hosts in the eyes of the world.

Disadvantages

- Security and the risk of terrorist attack.
- Boycotts and protests for political reasons.
- High costs and expenses to provide facilities and security.

Activities

1 How many of the activities that you are involved in at school are also Olympic sports or activities? Remember to include extra-curricular ones as well.

2 Carry out a study of the Olympic Games as a topic and look at the ways it has been used for political purposes in recent times.

Study tip

You will not be asked about any one particular Olympic Games, but you are likely to be tested on issues relating to them and the advantages and disadvantages of hosting them.

11.3 Competitions

One of the greatest appeals of taking part in physical activity is that it offers an element of competition and there are various ways that this is organised and arranged.

Knockouts

This is quite a simple format as it just involves one team playing against another with the winner going on to the next round and the loser dropping out of the competition. Most knockouts are played in rounds and can even have **seeded** teams or players. It is a very common form of competition and used in nearly all of the major sports and games.

Advantages

- Quick and easy to organise.
- Can allow high numbers, as half drop out after each round.

Disadvantages

- If you lose, you only get to play one game.
- You may need to have qualifying events or **byes** to get to the right mathematical number in order to lose half the entry during each round.

Leagues

This is probably the most common of all forms of competition and involves all teams or competitors playing against each other, often twice over a period of time or 'season'.

Advantages

- Can cater for a large entry with several leagues.
- Ensures that everyone has the same number of games.
- All arrangements can be made in advance for fixtures to be set and tickets to be organised.

Disadvantages

- It goes on for a very long time, if you are in a lower league it can take years to get up into a higher one.
- You can end up with fixture congestion towards the end of a season.

Objectives

Look at the different types and levels of competition that are commonly available.

Consider the ways these competitions are organised and run.

Consider the advantages and disadvantages of the different competition formats.

Key terms

Seeded: the best players or teams are selected and kept apart in the early rounds.

Bye: a free passage into the next round of a knockout.

∞ links

This links in to international sporting events and the Olympic Games on pages 126–129, as it has to be decided what form of competition to run. This also links closely to the role of an organiser on pages 116–117.

A *Frank Lampard and Ashley Cole celebrate for Chelsea. The Premiership is one of the most popular leagues in the world and attracts very large crowds.*

Ladders

This is where there are a set number of players or teams on a list or 'ladder' and you can challenge people above you to games and then take up their higher place in the ladder if you win.

Advantages

- Well suited to sports such as squash, badminton or tennis.
- Very simple to run and administer.

Disadvantages

- Progress can be very slow.
- Only really suitable for a fairly small entry.

Combination events

These combine elements of some or all of the above. Qualifying competitions may be played in leagues and winners then proceed to further leagues or the knockout stage. Round-robin events can take place where everyone plays each other in a mini-league and then there is just a final at the end.

Advantages

- As many games as you like can be played.
- Teams may get more than one chance to qualify.
- They allow for a high number of teams to be involved.

Disadvantages

- They can take a long time to complete.
- There may be some 'meaningless' games where teams have already qualified for the next stage.

B   *Chris Adcock and Andrew Ellis competing at the Yonex All England Badminton Open. Badminton is an example of a sport suited to ladders.*

Activity

Find out how many different competition types are available within your school and which is the most popular. Why is this?

C   *All Black Tony Woodcock scoring the first try of the 2011 Rugby World Cup final against France. The Rugby World Cup is an example of a combination event that culminates in a final.*

Study tip

You may be set a scenario of a situation and asked for the most suitable form of competition to use with it. Therefore, it is vital to know the advantages and disadvantages of each.

In this chapter you have learnt:

✔ what the major international sporting events are and which are the most popular

✔ the range of high-profile sporting events that are available to compete in or watch

✔ about the Olympic Games in recent years and some of the events and problems associated with it

✔ what advantages and disadvantages have to be considered and taken into account when one of these events is organised and run

✔ the types and formats of competitions that are used and the advantages and disadvantages of each.

Revision questions

1 Which of the following sports does not have an official World Cup or world championship?
   a Tennis
   b Cricket
   c Rugby
   d Athletics

2 What is a test match? In which sports do these take place?

3 Why are major international sporting events so common and popular?

4 When did the first Summer Olympic Games take place?

5 Give an example of a political leader who used the Olympics to promote their own political ideas and briefly describe what these were.

6 What are 'boycotts' and when were they linked to particular Games?

7 What is meant by the policy of apartheid and how did this affect specific countries and specific Games?

8 Describe two advantages that could be gained by hosting the Olympics or any other major event.

9 Describe two disadvantages that could result through hosting the Games or any other major event.

10 Briefly describe what is meant by a knockout competition.

11 How would you organise and arrange a knockout competition that had 36 entries? Work out all of the rounds that would have to be played right up to the final.

12 Explain two main advantages of the league format for competitions.

12 Social factors

■ Aims

✔ Be aware of the different formats of the media and the ways in which they cover sport.

✔ Understand the influences the media may have and the positive and negative effects that result.

✔ Understand the role that sponsors can play.

✔ Be aware of the influences that sponsors and sponsorship have.

✔ Understand the importance of role models and the influences that they can have.

✔ Have an outline and guide to health and safety.

✔ Know the rules relating to sport and equipment.

✔ Understand how science has been influential in sport.

✔ Know the role that ICT plays in sport.

This chapter looks at the different influences in society that affect physical education and sport in its widest sense. It also looks at the importance of ensuring that all physical activity is carried out safely, following all the guidelines and specific rules.

The first four sections are closely linked to the previous chapter on international sport as the media is hugely influential and to some degree dependent on the high profile that sport and some specific events enjoy. Similarly, the massive financial influence of sponsorship by the majority of the world's multinational companies, particularly sports goods manufacturers, is also a major and important issue.

Owing to the high profile of sport, there are an increasing number of role models who are highly influential in terms of lifestyle, attitudes and behaviour. This influence links closely to roles of media and sponsorship.

Sport is developing at an increasingly rapid rate and technology, through science and ICT, is moving rapidly in all aspects of provision, including the effects on officials, equipment, facilities and the organisation of sport.

12.1 The role of the media

The media is the main form of communication about sport and the types that have the greatest influence on sport are outlined below.

■ Television

This is one of the most powerful and commonly accessed form of the media and it transmits as **digital** and as **analog**. The introduction of digital transmissions, together with the introduction of satellite broadcasting, led to a huge increase in output of televised sport and providers were even able to introduce dedicated sport channels for the first time. The first totally dedicated sports channel was Sky Sports 1, which was first transmitted in 1991. There are now a very large number to choose from. There are specific rules about the transmission of sport on television, which are set by the government. For example, 'listed events' cannot be shown exclusively on '**pay per view**' or satellite and cable networks, such as the FA Cup Final, the Wimbledon Championship and the Olympic Games.

A *Events are broadcast all around the world live through the technology of satellite broadcasting*

■ Radio

There have been developments in radio broadcasting, just as there have been in television. The introduction of DAB (Digital Audio Broadcasting) has led to a growth in the number of radio stations broadcasting, to the extent that there are now dedicated sports channels on the radio just as there are on television. Radio has some distinct advantages over television in terms of broadcasting.

- Broadcasting costs are much lower as it only requires one commentator and the basic technology to transmit the broadcast.
- Radios are now very cheap, portable and easily accessible, so it is possible to listen in the car or while walking around.

Key terms

Digital: high-quality images and sounds that are converted into a digital signal with several stations at the same time.

Analog: a basic single signal, usually transmitted and received by an aerial.

Pay per view: where you pay for and watch one specific event or broadcast at a time.

Activity

Carry out a survey to look at all the different ways sport is covered on television, such as live matches, news bulletins and so on. See how many different formats you can come up with.

■ Press

Newspapers

Daily newspapers and the weekend publications both always have dedicated sports sections and it has become traditional for all sports news to be contained in the back sections.

Magazines

General magazines, including those given away as supplements on Sundays, often carry sports-related stories and topics and there are an increasing number of specialist magazines catering for specific sports.

Books

These can range from novels with sporting themes to textbooks (such as this one!) and even sporting autobiographies.

B *David Beckham signing a copy of his sporting autobiography*

■ Information technology

This is the most recent addition to the forms of the media and there is a wealth of information available on CD-ROMs or by accessing the internet where countless thousands of websites are available. There is also an increasing number of internet sites where television and radio broadcasts can be received.

⦿⦿ links

All of these forms of media are closely linked to international sport in Chapter 11, as they all cover the major events as they are performed.

Study tip

Being able to identify exactly what the media is and what it consists of is a common topic, but you will also need to know specific advantages each may have over the others.

12.2 The influence of the media

The power of the media is definitely not to be underestimated and there is no doubt that it is very influential in many ways. These can be broadly broken down into positive influences and negative ones.

Positive influences

Owing to the close link the media has with sport, there are many positive influences.

- *Demonstrating performance and participation* – showing high standards of performance, often with slow-motion replays to emphasise good points, cannot only make sure that individuals are well-informed, but it can also give them an **exemplar** to follow. Showing a lot of physical activity, promoting it and highlighting all of the health benefits associated with it promotes a much higher level of popularity and participation.

- *Increasing revenue* – the media supports sport directly through payments for broadcasting rights, as well as indirectly as sponsors are more likely to be involved if there is a high level of media coverage.

○○ links

This links particularly to health, fitness and a healthy active lifestyle in Chapter 5, as well as to school and physical education in Chapter 7 and the forms of the media on pages 134–135.

A *The sport of gymnastics has a surge in popularity, interest and participation every four years following the Olympic Games, which raises its profile*

B *Photographers are usually given the most popular areas to set up their equipment to ensure they get the best pictures*

- *Encouraging variety* – the very different types of output, such as informative, educational, instructive and entertainment, ensure that there is a great deal of variety in media coverage, which caters for all tastes.

Negative influences

The media do not set out to have negative influences on sport, but there are occasions when they do occur.

- *Intrusion on an event* – lots of photographers, reporters, cameras, cables and commentators can get in the way of spectators, as well as meaning a lack of privacy for the competitors.
- *Media pressure* – sometimes rules of competitions or events might be changed after media pressure to make something more dramatic or even to speed things up. The tie break in tennis was introduced partially for this reason.
- *Edited coverage* – television directors choose what is actually broadcast so not all of the action might be seen.
- *Altered event timings* – this is particularly the case with television, which needs to televise events to the largest audiences – this is usually the US market as it is very influential.
- *Undermining officials* – decisions made by officials can be undermined with slow-motion replays at stadiums.
- *Limited attendance* – if an activity is being televised, especially a live broadcast, then it can discourage people from attending the event.
- *Biased popularity* – activities attracting large media interest tend to flourish and grow, whereas those that do not can decline in popularity.

Key terms

Exemplar: a particularly good example or model of how something should be performed.

Media pressure: the way the media may hound or intrude upon individuals.

Activity

Find out about any other rule changes that might have been introduced due to media pressure, as well as any unusual start times for events, which also might have been influenced by the media.

Study tip

The positive and negative effects the media can have are common topics for questions, but you will need to give some up-to-date examples of these.

12.3 The role of sponsors

Sponsors and sponsorship are now closely linked with sport and are a significant influence and source of revenue.

◼ The range and scope of sponsorship

Individuals

Increasingly, sportspeople are negotiating individual sponsorship deals, many of them with more than one sponsor. Formula One racing drivers have almost every part of their overalls sponsored by various companies, while tennis authorities even have rules about the size and number of **logos** that can be placed on tennis tops. Quite simply, the individuals are paid money just to display the sponsor's name, wear a particular brand of sports clothing or footwear, or use a particular product such as a racket, ball or bat. As well as being paid to **endorse** goods, the individuals will be provided with all of these free of charge.

A *Jenson Button has to do a lot of promotional work. Very few sections of a Formula One driver's overalls are not taken up with some form of sponsorship logo.*

Objectives

Consider the way in which sponsors are involved in sport.

Consider the range and scope of sponsorship.

Consider the 'ease' of obtaining sponsorship and the benefits for the sponsors.

Key terms

Logo: the badge or emblem that a company uses as the representation of the company name.

Endorse: giving approval or support to something.

◯◯ links

Individuals in sport and sponsorship links closely with role models on pages 142–143.

Activity

1 Find out who is the highest paid sportsperson in terms of sponsorships and endorsements. Make a list of the sponsors who contribute to this. Also, carry out the same exercise for the most endorsed and sponsored sport.

Teams and clubs

Even school football teams attract sponsorship for their kit and major clubs are able to negotiate lucrative financial deals with sponsors for kit, equipment and even to provide a playing ground with the sponsor's name on it! Again, payments are made as part of this sponsorship at the top level, as well as providing all the goods free.

B *The Arsenal stadium is named the Emirates Stadium after their main sponsors who helped to finance the building of the stadium*

Activity

2 Find out who the official sponsors were of the most recent Olympic Games. If possible, find out how much money they contributed as sponsors.

Sports

Most sports have arranged sponsorship deals and will have a major sponsor associated with them to promote their leagues or competitions. Football, for instance, has sponsors for all of the major leagues as well as separate sponsors for the various cup competitions. However, some lesser known sports may not find it so easy to obtain this level of sponsorship and will certainly find long-term sponsors more difficult to find.

∞ links

There is a clear link here with international sport in general in Chapter 11, as well specifically with competitions on pages 130–131.

Events

Events are becoming increasingly popular with sponsors as they are then able to name the event after themselves for additional publicity. The Olympic Games attracts a huge number of sponsors and even publishes an official list of all of them. In return, the companies can use the Olympic Games logo on their products to increase sales. Events such as the London Marathon will get a major sponsor for the event itself and then others to provide the drinks, thermal blankets and so on.

■ Benefits for sponsors

The main benefit for all sponsors is to increase their revenue through advertising, improved sales or use of their product. They can also benefit by being associated with something, or someone, that is successful, topical, who has a good image and is thought to promote good health.

Study tip

One of the most common questions is about who or what can be sponsored, as well as the form the sponsorship is likely to take, such as equipment, payment or travel.

12.4 The influence of sponsorship

Sponsors only get involved in sport to have some kind of influence, which is primarily to promote their product. They will get involved in different ways and may have negative effects as well as positive ones.

Types of sponsorship

This can vary greatly and individuals, teams or sports may benefit from just one type or many.

- *Equipment* – this ranges from tennis rackets and golf balls right through to specialised training equipment such as a running treadmill.
- *Clothing* – some of this may be very basic, such as tracksuits or shirts, but other sports such as fencing require specific clothing, which can be quite expensive.
- *Accessories* – many performers will be paid to wear watches or even sunglasses, which are not related to their sport, as an advertising opportunity.
- *Transport and travel* – this can include flights, free cars or petrol or courtesy drivers.
- *Training* – facilities can be provided, personal trainers employed or even specific training equipment provided.
- *Entry fees and expenses* – these would all be covered and in the expenses all accommodation costs would also be paid, including hotel bills.

Unacceptable sponsorship

This is mainly anything associated with tobacco products or smoking, as this is clearly not a healthy link, encouraging something that is clearly established as life threatening. Most smoking sponsorship has now been banned by law and is illegal. Other examples can include alcoholic drinks, especially in activities including young people where the short- and long-term dangers of alcohol abuse would be an unfortunate association.

Increasingly, certain food types and particularly 'junk foods' are also being seen as unacceptable on health grounds.

Objectives

Consider the types of sponsorship that sponsors provide.

Consider some aspects of sponsorship that might not be acceptable.

Look at the advantages and disadvantages of sponsorship.

A *Michelle Wie is an established golfer, but golf equipment can be very expensive. A set of clubs provided by a sponsor can be a great help to an aspiring golfer*

∞links

This links with diet in Chapter 4 and health, fitness and healthy lifestyle in Chapter 5, specifically pages 58–59, as well as health and diet issues on pages 94–95. General links with sponsorship are also covered on pages 138–139.

Activity

Find out about any other sports that were previously allowed to be sponsored by tobacco companies. When and why was this stopped?

B   *The World Snooker Championship was previously known as the Embassy World Championship until the use of the sponsor was banned*

Advantages and disadvantages of sponsorship

Almost all sports actively seek sponsorship because of its advantages, but there can be unwelcome disadvantages too.

Advantages

- Sportspeople can concentrate on their sport without financial worries.
- Sports can be promoted and successful.
- Competitions can be bigger and better.
- The profile and image of the sport can be raised.
- Sponsors will get increased advertising, revenue, image, **goodwill** and even **tax relief**.

Disadvantages

- Sponsors may 'take over' the sport and start to dictate rule changes, clothing requirements or even the timings of events because of their media links.
- If the image of the sport is damaged, the sponsor can withdraw support.
- **Minority sports** find it difficult to attract sponsors.

> **Key terms**
>
> **Goodwill:** a good relationship and popularity.
>
> **Tax relief:** the payment of less tax.
>
> **Minority sports:** lesser known sports with lower participation levels.

> **Study tip**
>
> You might well be examined on the types of sponsorship and the advantages and disadvantages. You might also be asked for examples, particularly of unacceptable forms of sponsorship.

12.5 Role models

Just as in any other form of life, sport creates its own role models and they can be extremely influential, particularly on young people.

A role model is someone who other people might aspire to be like, who they look up to and who is seen as a good example to follow. Many sporting stars are excellent role models because of this, but they often have very short periods of influence as each generation tends to create their own role models.

■ Common characteristics

A role model needs to be someone who others will look up to, so the qualities they show are expected to be good ones, such as:

- competing or playing fairly and by the rules
- being **inspirational**
- being a good level performer in their own right and successful and famous through this
- setting trends for others to follow – in their own sport, another sport they clearly follow or endorse, or in the ways they go about competing
- shaping attitudes by the way they conduct themselves in their sporting life as well as in their private life

Objectives

Consider the characteristics that a role model might have.

Look at the importance of role models in setting participation trends or shaping attitudes.

Consider the effect role models can have on the popularity of activities.

Key terms

Inspirational: being able to motivate and fill someone with the urge to do something.

Ethnic: a group of people with a common national or cultural tradition.

Status: a level, rank or particular social position.

A *Tanni Grey-Thompson has been an inspirational role model as an athlete, a disabled performer and as an ambassador of sport*

- being accessible – this may mean that a young person sees the role model as someone they can access owing to the high level of media coverage that person has, or it may be someone far closer to them such as a family member or even their PE teacher
- taking part in a popular activity, or at least one that is growing in popularity
- representing a particular group, such as an **ethnic** group, a gender group or even a disability.

Pressure on role models

Any role model lives their life in the media spotlight and while this is probably the greatest pressure, there can be others, including:

- media pressure and lack of privacy owing to the high profile the individual has
- possible 'targeting' by other performers to attempt to damage their image
- being sought after and then dropped by companies cashing in on their role-model image
- being expected to be available to promote and increase participation levels in particular activities or sports
- the pressure of their **status** affecting their ability to perform at the highest level owing to other commitments
- the difficulty of coping with unexpected fame and money and being able to handle this.

Activities

1 Carry out a survey of your group to find out who is the most important role model for each person. Find out why this person is so inspirational.

2 Check the national papers for one week and see how many sporting role models are featured in non-sporting situations.

links

There are clear links here with the role and influence of media and of sponsorship on pages 134–141 as role models owe their fame to media coverage.

Study tip

The influence of role models is a very common topic and will usually relate to how it may be able to increase level of participation and performance in a sport or activity. You should be able to give an example of a current role model.

B *Being famous and being a role model also comes with its own pressure and lack of privacy*

12.6 Health and safety

This is one of the most important factors linked to your course and it is important to know the theory behind health and safety guidelines as well as ensuring that you apply these guidelines whenever you take part in any physical activity. These rules all apply for the wellbeing of yourself and of others.

■ General rules

There are specific legal requirements to ensure that health and safety is enforced. In PE in particular, there is a need for **risk assessments** to be carried out and all the necessary precautions to be put in place to minimise risk. The following precautions are those that you need to make in all cases.

Physical preparation

This can include warming-up correctly to prepare your body but it will also mean removing all jewellery, such as watches, earrings, bracelets and necklaces – PE teachers are legally required to make you do this. You may also be required to wear specific equipment, such as shin pads in the case of football for example. As part of this preparation, you might also need to carry out some training prior to taking part – taking part in a marathon run without having done any training prior to it will almost certainly result in injury or physical damage.

Environment

The playing environment must always be checked to make sure it is safe. This includes checking the playing surface and area. If it is an outdoor area, you need to check that there is no glass (crucial in jumping pits) or sharp objects. If it is an indoor area, then you need to make sure the surface is not slippery and that there are no other

A Putting on shin pads and wearing them throughout the game is essential when playing football

dangers, such as equipment left out or in the way. Certain weather conditions can be dangerous – frost can mean that the ground is too hard to play on or playing courts can be icy and slippery, and golf tournaments have to be interrupted during thunder storms because of the dangers of lightning. There have even been occasions when good weather causes problems – prolonged dry and sunny periods can mean that school pitches cannot be used for rugby because they are too hard.

Correct techniques

Each sport has its own specific techniques that must be used – a slide tackle is quite acceptable in soccer, but totally inappropriate in rugby!

B *Gloucester's Billy Twelvetrees goes in for a tackle against Richard Wigglesworth of Saracens. Tackling correctly in rugby is essential if you and your opponent are going to be as safe as possible.*

Lifting and carrying

The general rule for this is quite straightforward and applies in all cases. When lifting, you should bend the knees and keep the back straight to make sure the object you carry is kept close to the body. Repeat this action when lowering and do not attempt to lift something that is clearly too heavy on your own.

Activity

Find out how many different types of weather or climate conditions have caused stoppages or even postponements of sporting events at your school.

links

More detailed sport and equipment rules for particular activities are covered on pages 146–147.

Study tip

You need to be aware of the general rules that apply at all times. There are often questions relating to lifting and lowering that can be related to particular equipment used in PE lessons.

12.7 Sport and equipment rules

All sports have their own rules (although some sports call theirs laws or regulations), which make sure that the activity is played fairly and correctly but also safely to prevent injury. All schools make use of a 'play safe' policy that ensures each activity taught is done so correctly and in line with all the legal requirements and safety **legislation**.

Objectives

Consider some general sport rules relating to safety.

Consider some specific sporting examples of safety and guidance.

Consider some general and specific rules relating to footwear, clothing and equipment.

Activity

Find one example of a sport that is governed by rules, another that is governed by regulations and another that is governed by laws.

In all activities the following have to be considered.

Clothing

In most activities you are given fairly general guidelines about what to wear, but for some activities there is more guidance, for example:

- *Trampoline* – you should not wear loose clothing as there is the danger of it getting caught in the equipment.
- *Outdoor pursuits* – owing to **climatic** conditions you might need to wear waterproof clothing or several layers of warm clothing. If you were going surfing you would expect to wear a wetsuit, but for swimming you would wear a lightweight swimming costume that would not soak up lots of water and make floating difficult.

Footwear

Many activities have specific guidance about footwear and while a pair of trainers will do for most sports, there are activities where specialist footwear needs to be worn. These are for safety reasons, to ensure correct grip and protection.

- *Athletics* – spiked running shoes are needed on the track, but a marathon runner needs specific running shoes.
- *Games* – players need studded boots for football, rugby and hockey if played on grass and specialist shoes for artificial surfaces. Basketball players need trainers that offer extra ankle protection and squash and tennis players want light trainers that do not slow them down. All of them need footwear that fits well and is comfortable to avoid the main hazard of blisters!
- *Gymnastics* – gymnasts often compete in bare feet, or some very light gymnastics shoes (trampolinists have slightly different ones), and dancers need specialist shoes as well.

A *In netball, there is a rule that all players must have the length of their fingernails checked by the umpire before the game can start!*

links

This links closely to guidance on risk and challenge on pages 22–23.

Equipment

There are a great many regulations for this and they exist in almost every sport.

■ *Cricket* – all batters up to the age of 18 should wear a full-face helmet for protection. In addition to this there might be pads, gloves, thigh pads, arm guards and a chest pad.

■ *Hockey* – a game cannot start unless the goalkeeper is wearing a helmet and faceguard. In addition they should have pads, **kickers** and gloves.

Key terms

Legislation: laws, rules or regulations that are legally enforced.

Climatic: relating to the weather or particular weather conditions.

Kickers: protective hockey footwear that fits on over boots.

B *This hockey goalkeeper is wearing all the required protective equipment – helmet, faceguard, pads, kickers and gloves*

⬯links

Scientific developments in equipment are also considered on pages 148–149.

Study tip

Most questions on this topic will relate to being able to identify a specific safety aspect relating to an activity or a specific rule regarding the clothing, equipment or footwear that should be used.

12.8 Science in sport

The contribution that science has made in sport is far reaching and the advances that science has made through **technology** has benefited sport tremendously. Science has enabled improvements to be made, raised standards and greatly improved safety. The following are the main ways and areas that these developments have been achieved.

Equipment

The development of new materials has meant that many sports now have lighter, stronger and more durable equipment than they had in the past.

- Rackets in tennis, badminton and squash are now made using advanced engineering materials such as fibreglass, Kevlar® and titanium, which are polymers and alloys. These have all replaced the original wooden rackets.
- Pole-vaulters originally used bamboo poles but now use ones made of fibreglass or carbon fibre.
- Cricketers now wear pads made of high density compressed foam, which is up to 50 per cent lighter than previous equipment.
- Cyclists have specific bikes for different events made of very strong, lightweight materials and wear **aerodynamically** designed helmets.

Materials

The development of synthetic materials has revolutionised sportswear.

- *Swimming* – full-body suits were developed for swimmers to wear. They reduced the drag of the water as **streamlining** was improved. However, in 2010 the governing body of swimming (FINA) decided to ban them in all professional competitions as they felt they gave some competitors an unfair advantage. This is an example of an advance in technology that was so significant its use was banned.
- *Surfaces* – these have been rapidly improved. The choices are now between synthetic turf, synthetic fibre grass blades and rubber and sand granule infills for artificial surfaces for tennis, hockey and athletics. This means the AstroTurf™ surface is relatively outdated.
- *Footwear* – designs make use of composite materials that combine synthetic and natural materials, such as foam-blown polyurethane and kangaroo leather (in football boots), to provide strength and flexibility.

A *Cyclists such as the USA's Sarah Hammer have benefited from technology through lighter, stronger bikes and specially designed helmets*

B *Full-length body suits made from polyurethane and neoprene appeared in 2008 and greatly improved swimming times. The American Michael Phelps and others experienced the benefit of such scientific advances, breaking many world and Olympic records before the suits were banned in 2010.*

links

This links particularly with health and safety on pages 144–145, risk and challenge on pages 22–23 and with ICT in sport on pages 150–151. There has also been an effect on international sport, covered in Chapter 11.

Facilities

- Gymnasts used to have to perform in gymnasiums and sports halls, but now they use purpose-built facilities with recessed areas for safety pits.

- Tennis clubs now have specifically designed indoor areas where play is possible all year round instead of just in the summer months.

- Stadiums now have retractable roofs with air conditioning and humidity controls to allow the best possible competing conditions.

- Fitness gyms now have state-of-the-art equipment that is designed for particular muscles or muscle groups. They also have constantly updated cardiovascular equipment that has built-in monitors for recording heart rates and recovery times.

Study tip

It is important to keep up-to-date with technological advances as these happen very quickly and frequently. Having an up-to-date example to give in any exam question can be very beneficial.

12.9 ICT in sport

ICT has had a huge impact in sport and it is a rapidly advancing area that is constantly evolving.

Data recording and storage

Using computers means that vast amounts of data can be stored, analysed and presented in various ways, such as in spreadsheets. This is at all levels enabling individuals (such as GCSE PE students), schools (especially PE departments) and professional sports to make use of this facility. More and more programmes are being developed to enhance its use.

Performance analysis

Software and hardware is being developed to enable quite sophisticated levels of recording and analysis of performances. These systems are now commonly available in many schools. Systems such as Kandle and Dartfish both make use of video recording and playback, including many extra features such as **déjà vu** and sports motion analysis, which enable performers to track and view their own performances to gain **feedback** and even to be shown simultaneously with an exemplar.

Professional football clubs make use of ProZone™, which is a match analysis tool that can review previous games, analyse an individual player, carry out sectional analysis (such as looking at the defensive unit) and give a physical analysis (distances run, passes completed, etc.).

Even at a basic level, digital cameras using still photographs or brief video clips together with video cameras can record and allow playback of performances, which can then be reviewed. Being able to slow down the action, fast forward it and even rewind it can add to the value of the analysis and allow performers to see what they have done and consider ways they can improve. The fact that this is digital imagery that can be stored and reviewed later makes it an even more useful tool.

Objectives

Consider the impact that ICT has had on sport.

Consider the uses and benefits that ICT can bring.

Consider some of the practical applications that have been made of ICT.

Key terms

Déjà vu: where a performance action is replayed back on a time delay to enable the performer to review it constantly.

Feedback: information received as a basis for improvement.

Trajectory: the path or flight pattern of an object moving through the air.

∞ links

The aspects of performance analysis and the use of feedback links closely to components of fitness and skill-related factors of fitness on pages 70–71 and 72–73, as well as training in Chapter 6.

A *The déjà vu function of a video analysis system allows performers to gain instant feedback on their performance*

■ Performance aids

There are many ways in which ICT is aiding levels of performance, including the following:

- ■ *Fitness monitoring* – devices can now monitor heart rate, blood pressure and training zones to give a performer constant readouts and even advice.
- ■ *Hawk-Eye* – this is being used in tennis and cricket quite regularly to help with decision-making by tracking the flight and **trajectory** of balls.
- ■ *Video officials* – these are used in sports to check incidents and support decisions with wireless transmission links to the officials from their reviewing booths.

C   *The use of Hawk-Eye is becoming increasingly popular in tennis and cricket to aid decision-making*

B   *Referees such as Chris White are able to get the video officials to review action to help them to make the correct decision*

In this chapter you have learnt:

✔ about the role and influence of the media

✔ to consider the role and influence of sponsors and sponsorship

✔ to understand the importance of role models and the influences they may have

✔ about health and safety guidelines and the safeguards that must be taken

✔ that there are rules relating to particular sports and activities

✔ to be aware of the influence and impact that science is having on sport

✔ to be aware of the influence and impact that ICT is having on sport.

Revision questions

1 Which of the following is not a format of the media?

a Internet

b Press

c Video recorders

d Television

2 Describe four different ways in which television includes sport in transmissions.

3 What advantages might digital broadcasts have over analog broadcasts?

4 What advantages might radio coverage of an event have over televising the same event?

5 Using examples, describe two positive influences that the media can have on sport or sporting events.

6 What is the main advantage that sponsors are able to provide?

7 Describe three ways a sponsor might assist a sportsperson.

8 What are the advantages sponsors might gain through sponsoring an event?

9 What is meant by a role model?

10 How can role models influence young people?

11 Describe three general health and safety rules that should be applied at all times.

12 Choose a specific sport and describe two rules that apply to that sport to ensure safe participation.

13 Describe a way in which science technology has helped to improve performances in a sport or activity.

14 Describe three practical ways in which ICT has improved an aspect of sport.

13 Controlled assessment

This is the name given to the practical work that you carry out on the course and it is the assessment that your teachers will make regarding your levels of performance. The AQA examination group check these marks and also arrange moderation visits. When these moderation visits take place, the examination board sends a visiting moderator to watch the GCSE PE pupils perform. This person works closely with the PE staff to make sure that all the marks being awarded are accurate and correct.

You will be assessed according to which qualification you are being entered for. These are the number of controlled assessments for each:

- Short Course – two assessments, from two of the activity groups. At least one must be as a player (or performer).
- Full Course – four assessments, from at least two activity groups. At least two must be as a player (or performer).
- Double Award – four assessments (these must be different from those you may have had assessed in the Full Course so they will really be four additional assessments) from at least three activity groups.

You will be assessed and marked under Key Processes A, B and C. These are explained over the next two pages.

Developing skills in physical education

There are a maximum of 10 marks available for this. In this part of your practical work the emphasis is on how well you are able to develop and apply the skills or techniques that apply to each particular activity. To get the highest marks, you will be asked to apply these skills or techniques in increasingly difficult or demanding situations. This might mean that some drills or practices become harder or that you are asked to take part in some conditioned games where some of the rules are changed or adjusted.

You will be challenged to try more difficult and higher-quality skills and techniques and you will be marked on your levels of consistency when performing with precision, control and fluency.

Being creative and making decisions

There are a maximum of 10 marks available for this. In this part of your practical work the emphasis is on how well you take part in the actual game or physical activity. You will be asked to demonstrate your ability to anticipate the responses of others (if you are in a team situation or involved with opponents), as well as showing how you select and apply your skills, tactics and compositional ideas within your own performance. To get the highest marks, you will be assessed on your levels of consistency and effectiveness in the full, recognised version of the game or event.

You will be challenged to show how well you can select and use tactics, strategies and compositional ideas imaginatively in circumstances that may become more complex and demanding. You will also need to show that you can respond to these changing circumstances as they arise during the performance.

A *Your performance levels in various different practical roles will be marked in your controlled assessment*

Key process C

Evaluating and improving

There are a further 10 marks available for this part of your practical performance, but you will only be asked to do this for **one** of your chosen practical activities.

To gain these marks you have to show that you can analyse and judge a performance accurately, making some judgements using technical terms to comment on the strengths and weaknesses. You will also need to be able to take some action in order to improve the quality and effectiveness of this performance.

The task you will be given will either be to look at a performance, or consider your own, and then identify at least one strength and one weakness and fully explain it using the appropriate technical terms. To improve this performance you would need to consider some actions that could increase the strengths and diminish the weaknesses, taking action to tackle any apparent deficiencies. You will be required to carry out this work independently and without guidance from your teacher.

C   *You will be tested on a variety of skills in the controlled assessment*

B   *You will need to practice and develop skills and techniques as part of your controlled assessment*

13.1 Activity groups

You can choose activities from any of these six activity groups:

■ Group 1

Outwitting opponents, as in game activities. Success in this activity area can be achieved by overcoming opponents in competition by directly affecting each other's performance.

A *Rugby is an example of a Game Activity (Group 1) in which you are required to outwit opponents*

■ Group 2

Accurate replication of actions, phrases and sequences, as in gymnastic activities. Success in this activity area can be through the ability to repeat actions, phrases and sequences of movement as perfectly as possible.

B *Rhythmic gymnastics demonstrates the ability to repeat sequences and actions, required for gymnastic activities (Group 2)*

■ Group 3

Exploring and communicating ideas, concepts and emotions, as in dance activities. Success in this activity area can be achieved by a performer or choreographer expressing ideas, feelings, concepts and emotions by communicating artistic or choreographic intentions to an audience.

C *Street dance is part of the dance activities (Group 3)*

Group 4

Performing at maximum levels in relation to speed, height, distance, strength or accuracy, as in athletic activities. Success in this activity area can be achieved through personal best scores or times, and in competition with others' scores and times.

Group 5

Identifying and solving problems to overcome challenges of an adventurous nature, as in lifesaving, personal survival in swimming and outdoor and adventurous activities. Success in this activity area can be achieved by overcoming challenges effectively and safely.

D *Group 4 (athletic activities) are activities which can require performance at maximum speed, such as swimming*

Group 6

Exercising safely and effectively to improve health and wellbeing, as in fitness and health activities. Success in this activity area can be achieved through improved feelings of health, fitness and wellbeing.

There are a large number of activities that may be available in these six groups and there are 99 specific activities listed in the exam documentation, so it is very likely that any activity you are involved in can be considered for assessment. You will need to check with your teacher to see which of the areas it may come under and also whether or not it is a recognised activity so that you may gain marks for it.

You must remember that you have the option within these groups to be an actual player (or performer) in the activity, dependent on which exams you are being entered for in the identified roles.

E *Outdoor and adventurous activities (Group 5), including climbing, need you to overcome challenges of an adventurous nature*

F *Fitness and health activities (Group 6), such as aqua aerobics, are designed to improve health and wellbeing*

When you are being assessed in Units 2, 4 and 6 you will be doing so either as a player or a performer. You will be required to perform across a number of the six activity groups (see 13.1). This section outlines what is required of your performance in each of these groups.

■ Group 1: outwitting opponents

You are likely to be a player if you are being assessed in this group, but you could also be a performer if you are taking part in a combat activity such as tae kwon do. When you are a player you might have the option of playing in different positions, such as a midfielder in an invasion game. You might also take on specialist positions, such as a goalkeeper in hockey and soccer or a wicketkeeper in cricket.

■ Group 2: accurate replication of actions, phrases and sequences

If you are assessed in this Group, you will have to compose and perform three short sequences for key process A and two longer sequences for key process B. There are some very specific instructions about the ways in which these sequences must be designed, their duration, and the skills, actions and techniques which must be included. Make sure that you are fully aware of all of these before you start working on them!

A   *Being a player/performer in Group 1 focuses on outwitting opponents, which can be as part of a huge variety of activities. Many team games are accepted (for example soccer, hockey and netball), as well as more individual combative sports such as fencing (pictured).*

Group 3: exploring and communicating ideas, concepts and emotions

As a performer assessed in this group, you will be asked to prepare and perform in three short sequences for key process A and perform in a group dance and either a solo or a duo/trio for key process B. These have to be a minimum of three minutes each, including complex techniques and choreographic devices. You will have to provide a brief explanation of the dance and identify your own particular contribution to the choreography.

Group 4: performing at maximum levels in relation to speed, height, distance, strength or accuracy

If you are being assessed in athletic activities, these must be from at least two different event groups and will involve you taking part in a minimum of three athletic competition meetings. Another aspect to this assessment will be improvement in times and distances, in relation to technique and different conditions. There are also more specific guidelines for weightlifting, swimming, cycling and target games, where accuracy will also be a crucial factor.

B *Performing in Group 4 activities can often involve athletic events*

Group 5: identifying and solving problems to overcome challenges of an adventurous nature

As a performer, you will have to take part in short routines for key process A and longer journeys/expeditions/procedures/rescues for key process B. You will need to show a degree of improvement in the context of conditions and degree of challenge. Guidance is given regarding the length of time for these challenges, which will differ among the different activities.

Group 6: exercising safely and effectively to improve health and wellbeing

As a performer being assessed in this group, you will have to prepare for, and participate in, sessions over a sufficient amount of time. The ways in which you perform the exercises, safety aspects, and attitude will all be considered. You will also have to be able to devise and implement effective and appropriate warm-ups and cool-downs.

C *Canoeing is an example of an activity in Group 5. Different types of water can count as contrasting terrains.*

13.3 Organiser

This means that you take on the role of someone putting some sort of event or competition together and you have to come up with a written plan outlining what you intend to do. In order to do this properly you need to consider most of the following:

- What equipment might need to be provided or brought along.
- The times that your event or competition will be starting and finishing and how long particular parts of it would take up.
- The rules that will have to apply. You might want to have some slightly different ones or add some new ones. You will have to make sure that you have enough officials or judges to help you run the event and that they were also aware of all of the rules.

The second part of the process involves actually running the event and making sure that it all runs smoothly. This could include some of the following:

- Timekeeping, which you will have to control.
- Collecting and recording scores and results from the event and using these to come up with the final result or outcome.

There will be particular areas that you will be assessed on when you carry out this role, so it is important that you consider them carefully.

1 Your organisational skills, taking into account the amount of preparation and planning you carried out before the event started.

2 Your communication skills – this could be the way you wrote some instructions, as well as the way you spoke to the people involved, and your ability to make all of your instructions clear and understandable.

3 How you demonstrated your leadership skills to ensure that everything ran smoothly and that you were able to deal with any problems that might have cropped up unexpectedly.

4 The ways you were able to control the event once it was underway and how you made your presence felt as the person in charge.

5 The safety aspects involved in your event – you will have had to carry out a risk assessment (see pages 144 and 145 for further details regarding this) to make sure that everyone involved is able to perform in complete safety.

> ### Key process A
>
> As an organiser you will assessed according to your ability to plan an event, including written evidence of your planning, describing the playing/performing area (or areas), the equipment required, the times of the competition and the rules and judges (or officials) for the competition.

> ### Key process B
>
> To attain marks here, you will have to put your plans into action and then be assessed on your level of effectiveness in handling the process together with your ability to set up the competition or event. This may include timekeeping, collecting and collating the scores and producing the final result.

A *You will need the same skills, no matter what size the event you are organising!*

13.4   Leader/coach

In this role you take on leadership or coaching for a group of performers.

One of the tasks you will be set and assessed on is to warm-up a group of students, then observe, analyse and suggest improvements that could be made.

A further task, on which you will be assessed, is your ability to observe, analyse and suggest improvements to an individual performer, specifically on their skills and techniques.

There will be particular areas that you will be assessed on when you carry out this role, so it is important that you consider them carefully.

1   The amount of subject knowledge you can show regarding the activity you are leading/coaching. You will need to know the rules and the correct techniques if you are going to help someone to improve and spot any weaknesses.

2   You will have to show good communication skills, as you need to explain yourself and make sure members of the group clearly understand what you are telling them. You might need to use diagrams or some other way of communicating thoughts and ideas, such as recording/filming performances to make your points.

3   You will have to show that you can clearly analyse a performance, giving detailed information about what you have observed and what guidance/advice you can give to help the performer to improve.

4   The ways you were able to control the session, or sessions, once they were underway and how you made your presence felt as the person in charge will be assessed.

5   The safety aspects involved in your sessions – you will have had to carry out a risk assessment (see pages 144 and 145 for further details regarding this) to make sure that everyone involved is able to perform in complete safety.

Key process A

As a leader/coach you will be assessed on your ability to warm-up a group of students and observe, analyse and suggest improvements to an individual (someone who you would choose), based on assessing their particular skills and suggesting ways to improve or develop some core skills.

Key process B

To attain marks here you will need to show your ability to observe, analyse and suggest improvements to the individual you have identified regarding their skills and techniques, as well as leading or coaching the player in the full performance of the activity or situation.

A   *This coach is working with a group to help them improve their levels of performance*

This role can have a different name depending upon which type of activity you have chosen, such as referee/umpire (soccer or netball), judge (gymnastics or trampoline), marshal/steward (athletics or cross country) or scorer/timekeeper/recorder (basketball, cricket or athletics).

One of the most important qualities that you will need as an official is the ability to apply decision-making, including the following:

- Establishing control and ensuring there is the correct level of discipline maintained at all times.

- Making a decision about how severe each action might be, especially those that would count as rule infringements,

- Allowing advantages to progress as well as knowing when to impose specific penalties when they are required.

- Being consistent with decision-making and making sure that decisions are accurate at all times.

- Dealing with the pressure of being the person in charge, which can result in a high level of pressure.

There will be particular areas that you will be assessed on when you carry out this role, so it is important that you consider them carefully.

1 Your understanding of the rules of the particular activity, requiring you to keep up-to-date with the rules, understand signals that need to be shown and also be aware of some of the tactics that competitors might use.

2 Your communication skills such the use of your voice, possibly a whistle and the specific gestures and signals that apply to that particular activity.

3 Your ability to officiate effectively, including being correctly positioned, communicating with other officials (such as referee's assistants) and being fit enough to keep up with the play.

4 The ways in which you were able to control the match, game or competition once it was underway, and how you made your presence felt as the person in charge.

5 The safety aspects involved in your officiating sessions – you will have had to carry out a risk assessment (see pages 144 and 145 for further details regarding this) to make sure that everyone involved is able to perform in complete safety. You will need to enforce any particular safety rules that apply to your chosen activity (such as checking fingernails in netball).

Key process A

You will be assessed on your ability to explain the rules to a player (or performer) and officiate (or judge) the core skills/techniques in small-sided games or structured practices in the authentic context, such as set plays and dead-ball situations.

Key process B

You can attain marks here by showing your ability to officiate (or judge) a performance in the full performance or activity situation. Particular attention will be paid to your levels of control and presence, understanding of the rules (or composition), officiating (or judging) skills, communication skills and levels of consistency/effectiveness in identifying any rule infringements.

A *Officials need to control players and maintain discipline*

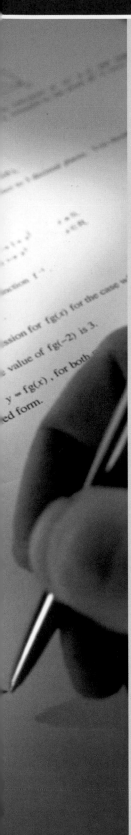

EXAMINATION SKILLS

Physical Education courses

This chapter considers the skills you will need to have in order to be able to successfully answer the question paper component of your examination.

The question papers vary depending upon which qualification you are being entered for, so you need to know which one it is and prepare accordingly.

There are three different qualifications and the format is as follows:

■ Short Course (Unit 1)

This is a 45-minute examination with a maximum mark of 40.

The question paper is divided up into three parts. Part 1 has five multiple choice questions, worth 1 mark each. Part 2 has short answer questions, worth 15 marks in total. Part 3 has questions based on a scenario, which is made available prior to the examination, and is worth a total of 20 marks. This is where your use of English will be assessed.

■ Full Course (Unit 3)

This examination lasts 1 hour 30 minutes with a maximum mark of 80.

The question paper is divided up into three parts. Part 1 has 10 multiple-choice questions, worth 1 mark each. Part 2 has short-answer questions, worth 30 marks in total. Part 3 has questions based on a scenario, which is made available prior to the examination, and is worth a total of 40 marks. This is where your use of English will be assessed.

■ Double Award (Unit 5)

This examination lasts 1 hour 30 minutes with a maximum mark of 70.

The question paper is in one continuous section. The final question is based on a scenario, which is made available prior to the examination. This is where your use of English will be assessed.

Double Award candidates should be aware that they also have to answer the Full Course question paper as Unit 3 of their examination.

It is very important that you know which qualification you have been entered for, that you know what types of questions you will be asked and that you practice answering these types of questions before the exam.

These are the more general points you should bear in mind:

- Multiple-choice questions always give you an option of four choices and you must circle the correct answer. These questions will either ask you to identify what **is** or what **is not** the correct answer, so be sure you know which one of these two has been asked for.

- Make sure that you read all of the questions very carefully and look for information in it which is designed to help you. Some words will be in **bold** type because they are key words, which you can underline or highlight to help you if you like. They are usually in one of two categories:

  1 **Give**, **state** or **name** – these usually need just a one-word answer or a brief answer.

  2 **Describe**, **explain** or **consider** – these require longer responses, which have to include reasons for your answer.

- All of the questions have gaps for you to put your answers in. These will give you some indication of the length your response needs to be.

- Question papers have bar codes on each page because they are scanned and then marked electronically. That is why you are asked to use a black ballpoint pen, so that the scanner can recognise it. You are also asked not to write outside of the margins. This is also to do with the scanner, and if you ignore this the marker will not see what you have written!

- Look at the number of marks that are available for the question. One mark means you could get away with a one-word answer, but for any more you are going to have to write more – probably at least one different point for each mark available.

- Check whether there are any examples asked for, as this is very common. You should be able to use many examples from your own experience, which will be perfectly acceptable. Try to make your example match your answer, rather than start with your example and then make your answer match that.

- You can use diagrams to help to explain an answer if you find it makes a point easier, but you must make sure that you label it clearly.

- Some specialist terminology is going to be used in the questions, so you need to know that you understand all the terms in the specification so that you understand what you are being asked. Also, try to use the correct terminology in your answers, as these are more likely to gain the marks.

- Pace yourself over the full time allowed for your paper as you have to answer all of the questions, but it is up to you what order you answer them in. You might decide to answer the questions you think are the easiest ones first.

- Check all your completed answers. Leave yourself some time at the end to do this and make sure that you are checking them against the questions set.

- Practise answering as many questions as possible before you take the real exam so that you improve your examination technique. You will find that the style of the questions remains the same even though the subject of the question may be different.

- The scenario question is worth the most marks and requires a longer response using 'continuous prose'. This means that you cannot use bullet points, but must use full sentences with correct punctuation. Remember that you will have been given the scenario in advance so you should be able to identify specific factors that have been highlighted and that are likely to have questions based on them.

Practice questions

The following pages have examples of the types of questions that will be set in the examination. There will be all three different styles on each of the question papers for the Short Course, Full Course and Double Award.

The multiple-choice questions and short-answer questions can be based on any of the content relating to the knowledge and understanding of the active participant, so all of the content needs to be covered and revised. The scenario questions will also be based on this content – not necessarily on all of it, but focused particularly on the aspects highlighted by the scenario.

The multiple-choice questions have a question with a choice of four possible correct answers numbered from a to d. You have to circle which you consider to be the correct one.

The short-answer questions are usually set in at least two parts and have blank lines for you to write your answers on before the mark total, which is shown at the bottom. You must be careful to not write outside the margins set as these papers will be electronically marked. As they have to be scanned into a computer, any writing outside the set area will not be detected.

The scenario questions have far more marks available for each question and you must use 'continuous prose', so you cannot answer in note form or by using bullet points. You will be assessed in this part of the question paper on your use of good English, ability to organise information clearly and use of appropriate specialist vocabulary.

For those who are taking the Double Award, there is an additional scenario question paper that is based on the additional theory content, which you need to have covered.

◼ You will now see examples of:

- Multiple-choice examples
- Short-answer question examples
- Scenario example
- Double Award scenario example.

Multiple-choice questions

The following are five examples of these types of question.

1   All of the following are somatotypes except:
   (a) Endomorph
   (b) Seisomorph
   (c) Ectomorph
   (d) Mesomorph   *(1 mark)*

2   Which of the following terms relates to the time spent training?
   (a) Specificity
   (b) Progression
   (c) Overload
   (d) Reversibility   *(1 mark)*

3   Other school subjects that might have some PE content in them are known as:
   (a) National Curricular
   (b) Extra-curricular
   (c) Cross-curricular
   (d) Semi-curricular   *(1 mark)*

4   All of the following would be considered to be acceptable forms of sponsorship except:
   (a) Sports goods manufacturers
   (b) Car manufacturers
   (c) Mobile phone companies
   (d) Cigarette companies   *(1 mark)*

5   Which acid can build up as a result of fatigue?
   (a) Formic
   (b) Hydrochloric
   (c) Citric
   (d) Lactic   *(1 mark)*

Short-answer questions

The following are five examples of these types of question.

1 Components of fitness are important for sports performers.
   (a) What is meant by the term 'balance'? Give **one** example from a physical activity. *(2 marks)*
   (b) What is meant by the term 'coordination'? Give **one** example from a physical activity. *(2 marks)*
   (Total 4 marks)

2 It is important to lift and carry equipment safely. **Describe** the technique that you should use when doing this. *(3marks)*
   (Total 3 marks)

3 Performers often use weight training as part of a range of training exercises.
   (a) State **one** benefit to fitness that can be achieved by the use of weight training. *(1 mark)*
   (b) In relation to weight training, what is the difference between 'repetitions' and 'sets'? *(2 marks)*
   (Total 3 marks)

4 Schools can promote and influence participation in physical education.
   (a) Describe how teachers can influence participation. *(2 marks)*
   (b) What is meant by 'extra-curricular' activities? Include **one** example in your answer. *(2 marks)*
   (Total 4 marks)

5 The amount of available leisure time has increased and this has had an effect on the leisure industry. Identify and explain **two** reasons why leisure time has increased.
   (a) Reason 1
   (b) Reason 2 *(Total 4 marks)*

Scenario questions

The following is an example of a scenario-based question, which would be part of the Short Course and the Full Course award.

These questions are linked to the scenario information, which is outlined prior to the examination and which is copied below.

Joanne is an elite-standard athlete who regularly competes at international level as a marathon runner.

She is 28 years old, married and has a one-year-old daughter. She has been regularly competing as an athlete since her early teens, when she showed potential as a runner. She represented her school at county level and then took part in and won the National Championships.

In her early career she only ran middle-distance races, specialising in the 1,500 metres. However, as she got older she increased the distances of her competitive runs.

Joanne lives in England, but she regularly travels abroad to train, and takes part in her sport full time after having had a brief career break for the birth of her daughter. She does not have another job and her income is based on sponsorship, winnings and appearance money for the events she attends. She has a full-time coach and also a manager. As an elite performer she also receives help and funding from the National Lottery.

1   Explain what particular relevance, if any, Joanne's age and the fact that she is a female might have on her ability to compete at the level she is at in her chosen sport. In your answer, describe what type of physique you would expect Joanne to have.

(8 marks)

Double Award scenario questions

The following is an example of a scenario-based question, which would be set for **Double Award candidates only**.

These questions are linked to the scenario information, which is released before the examination and copied below.

Tyrone Brown

Age: 16

Height: 1.63 m (5' 4")

Weight: 89 kg (14 stone)

Lives in a bungalow half a mile from school.

Favourite subject: ICT

Least favourite subject: PE, which he usually manages not to take part in as he has asthma and has a note from his mum.

Tyrone follows the same routine every day from Monday to Friday. He gets up at 8 am, has a shower and then has a full English breakfast. At 8.45 am either his mum or dad will drive him to school. On the way they stop at the shops and he buys sweets, chocolate bars and crisps to eat at break and lunchtimes. At break time Tyrone goes to the school canteen and gets a large slice of chocolate cake as he usually eats most of his chocolate bars between lessons.

1 pm is lunchtime and Tyrone has a packed lunch most days, which includes a pork pie, a pasty, cheese and ham sandwiches on white bread, a couple of cans of cola and two packets of crisps. On Fridays he has school dinner as it is chips day, and he usually has double chips, cheese and gravy. Tyrone spends the rest of his lunchtime sitting talking to friends, or he may go to the computer room.

After school Tyrone either gets picked up by his mum or dad or he gets the bus home. He likes getting the bus because then he can go to the chip shop and get fish and chips or sausage in batter and chips for his tea. Sometimes he goes to the local Indian takeaway and he orders a large lamb curry with chips. He eats it while he watches the television. When he has finished his mum clears away his plate, gets him another can of cola from the fridge and microwaves him chocolate pudding with chocolate sauce.

After tea he usually gets another can of cola and settles down to watch a film or play on his computer. He has a sandwich or a slice of cake. At the weekend he usually has a lie-in until lunch and often goes to the pub with his parents for lunch. On Saturday night he likes to have a Chinese takeaway; his favourite is sweet and sour pork. He also likes to have a roast dinner at the pub on Sunday with his parents. His favourite is roast beef with Yorkshire pudding followed by chocolate pudding.

(a) Explain **two** harmful effects Tyrone's diet is having on his health.   *(4 marks)*

(b) Explain **two** changes Tyrone should make to his diet.
   (**Answer in continuous prose**)
   (4 marks)

AQA Specimen paper 2009

Glossary

A

Accredited: a recognised standard of award leading on to a higher learning level.

Aerobic exercise: exercise carried out using a supply of oxygen.

Aerodynamic: shaped to reduce the drag of air passing over it.

Alveoli: small air sacs in the lungs where gaseous exchange takes place.

Ambidextrous: the ability to use both hands with equal levels of skill.

Analog: a basic single signal, usually transmitted and received by an aerial.

Antagonist: the muscle that relaxes to allow a movement to take place.

Apartheid: a policy of separating groups, especially because of race or colour.

Apprehensive: fearful about the future.

Articulation: a movable joint between inflexible parts of the body.

Athlete's foot: a fungal infection between the toes.

B

Basal metabolic rate: the minimum rate of energy required to keep all of the life processes of the body maintained when it is at rest.

Bespoke: designed for a particular individual.

Blood pressure: the force of the circulating blood on the walls of the arteries.

Body composition: the percentage of body weight that is fat, muscle and bone.

Body image: a personal concept of your own physical appearance.

Boycott: not using or dealing with something, as a protest.

Bronchitis: inflammation of the air passages between the nose and the lungs.

Bye: a free passage into the next round of a knockout.

C

Calorie: a unit that measures heat or energy production in the body.

Challenge: a test of your ability or resources in a demanding situation.

Climatic: relating to the weather or particular weather conditions.

Competitive: an activity that involves some form of contest, rivalry or game.

Concentric: when the muscle shortens (it also tends to bulge, such as the biceps in the arm).

Cross-curricular: linking with other subjects taught in school.

Culture: the ideas, customs and social behaviour of a particular people or society.

D

Dehydration: the rapid loss of water from the body.

Déjà vu: where a performance action is replayed back on a time delay to enable the performer to review it constantly.

Devout: devoted or dedicated to.

Digital: high-quality images and sounds that are converted into a digital signal with several stations at the same time.

Dilated: enlarged, expanded or widened.

E

Eccentric: when the muscle gradually lengthens and returns to its normal length and shape.

Economic wellbeing: having sufficient income for basic necessities.

Endorse: giving approval or support to something.

Equestrian: relating to horseback riding or horseback riders.

Equity: something that is fair, just and impartial.

Ethnic: relating to a group of people with a common national or cultural tradition.

Etiquette: the unwritten rules or conventions of any activity.

Exchequer: the government department that is in charge of the public revenues, also known as the treasury.

Exemplar: a particularly good example or model of how something should be performed.

Exercise: activity that requires physical or mental exertion, especially when performed to develop or maintain fitness.

Extra-curricular: an activity that takes place out of timetabled lessons, such as lunchtimes or after school.

Extrinsic reward: something that is done for a particular reward that is visible to others.

F

Fast: to eat only certain types of food or to reduce food intake.

Feedback: information received as a basis for improvement.

FIT: frequency, intensity and time are ways to make the body work harder.

Fitness: good health or good condition, especially as the result of exercise and proper nutrition.

Flexibility: the range of movement around a joint.

G

Gaseous exchange: the process where oxygen is taken in from the air and exchanged for carbon dioxide.

Gender: the particular sex of an individual.

General fitness: a state of general good health and to be able to carry out activities at a relatively low level.

Glycogen: the form of carbohydrate storage, which is converted into glucose as needed by the body to satisfy its energy needs.

Goodwill: a good relationship and popularity.

H

Heart rate: the number of times your heart beats in one minute, which is one contraction and relaxation of the heart.

Hijab: a head covering that must be worn in public by some Muslim women.

I

Inclusion: a policy that no one should experience barriers to learning as a result of their disability, heritage, gender, special educational need, ethnicity, social group, sexual orientation, race or culture.

Inherent: something you are born with.

Insertion: the end of the muscle attached to the bone that moves.

Inspirational: being able to motivate and fill someone with the urge to do something.

Intercostal muscles: abdominal muscles inbetween the ribs which assist in the process of breathing.

Intrinsic reward: something that gives a person an individual or internal satisfaction derived from doing something well.

J

Joint: a connection point between two bones where movement occurs.

K

Kickers: protective hockey footwear that fits on over boots.

Knowledge of performance: this relates to how well the performance was carried out rather than just the end result.

Knowledge of results: this is a form of terminal feedback at the end of a performance and could be as simple as winning or losing.

L

Lactic acid: a mild poison and waste product of anaerobic respiration.

Landscape: the aspect of the land characteristic of a particular region.

Laps: the number of times each set of stations is performed.

Legacy commitment: a plan to harness the enthusiasm generated by the London 2012 Olympics and to ensure it continues.

Legislation: laws, rules or regulations that are legally enforced.

Leisure industry: any provider that provides opportunities for people in their available leisure time.

Local muscular fatigue: when a muscle, or group of muscles, is unable to carry on contracting and movement stops.

Logo: the badge or emblem that a company uses as the representation of the company name.

Low impact: not strenuous with little or no pressure on the joints.

M

Maximal strength: the greatest amount of weight that can be lifted in one go.

Media: the various forms of mass communication, such as radio, TV and the press.

Media pressure: the way the media may hound or intrude upon individuals.

Mentors: influential, trusted and experienced advisers.

Metabolic: the whole range of biochemical processes that occur within us.

MHR: maximum heart rate (220 minus age).

Minority sports: lesser-known sports with lower participation levels.

Motivation: your drive to succeed and desire and energy to achieve something.

Movement time: how quickly a performer can carry out an actual movement.

Muscle tone: where tension remains in a muscle, even when it is at rest.

Musculature: the system or arrangement of muscles on a body.

N

Nutrients: the substances that make up food.

O

Open sport: an activity that allows both amateurs and professionals to compete together.

Origin: the end of the muscle attached to the fixed bone.

Overload: making the body work harder than normal in order to improve it.

P

Patella: the kneecap.

Pay per view: where you pay for and watch one specific event or broadcast at a time.

Peak: at your very best – the best prepared period for you to be able to perform.

Peer group: people of the same age and status as you.

Peer-group pressure: where the peer group will attempt to persuade an individual to follow their lead.

Performance-enhancing drugs: a type of unlawful drug that can help to improve sporting performance.

Periodisation: the different parts

of a training programme.

Physiology: the functions and processes of the human body.

Physique: the form, size and development of a person's body.

Plateauing: where progress seems to halt within a training programme and it takes some time to move on to the next level.

Power: the combination of speed and strength.

Prescription drugs: drugs that cannot be bought over the counter but only with a doctor's prescription.

Prime mover: the muscle that initially contracts to start a movement, also known as the 'agonist'.

Private enterprise: a privately owned business not regulated in the same way as a state-owned organisation.

Proficiency: being adequately or well qualified.

Progression: where training is increased gradually as the body adjusts to the increased demands being made on it.

Propaganda: messages aimed at influencing the behaviour or opinions of large numbers of people.

Pulse: a recording of the rate per minute at which the heart beats.

Q

Quadriceps: the group of four muscles on the upper front of the leg.

R

Reaction time: how quickly you are able to respond to something or some form of stimulus.

Recreational: any form of play, amusement or relaxation performed as games, sports or hobbies.

Repetition maximum (RM): the maximum weight you are able to lift once.

Repetitions: the number of times you actually move the weights.

Reversibility: if training stops, then the effects gained can be lost too.

Risk: the possibility of suffering harm, loss or danger.

Risk assessment: to look at the likelihood of damage, or the possible dangers involved, in carrying out a particular action or activity.

Role models: people who others might aspire to be like, they are looked up to and seen as good examples.

Rural areas: areas outside cities and towns.

S

Sedentary: sitting down or being physically inactive for long periods of time.

Seeded: the best players or teams are selected and kept apart in the early rounds.

Sets: the number of times you carry out a particular weight activity.

Shamateur: someone who competes in an amateur sport but who receives illegal payments.

Shuttle runs: running backwards and forwards across a set distance.

Somatypes: different body types based on shape, most commonly endomorph, mesomorph and ectomorph.

Specificity: training that is particularly suited to a particular sport or activity.

Sprains: the overstretching or tearing of ligaments at a joint.

Stations: particular areas where types of exercise are set up or performed.

Status: a level, rank or particular social position.

Sternum: the chest or breastbone.

Strains: the overstretching of a muscle, rather than a joint.

Streamline: designed to offer very little resistance to the flow of air or water.

Stress fractures: a break in the bone caused by repeated application of a heavy load or constant pounding on a surface, such as by running.

Synchronise: an adjustment that causes something to occur at the same time.

Synovial: where bony surfaces are covered by cartilage, connected by ligaments with a joint cavity containing synovial fluid.

T

Tactics: pre-arranged and rehearsed strategies or methods of play.

Talent: a special natural ability or aptitude.

Tax relief: the payment of less tax.

Technique: the manner or way in which someone carries out or performs a particular skill.

Technology: the application of science for practical purposes.

Tennis elbow: a painful injury or inflammation of the tendon attached to the elbow joint.

Test match: a match played in cricket or rugby by all-star teams from different countries.

Training threshold: the minimum heart rate to be achieved to ensure that fitness improves.

Training zone: the range of the heart rate within which a specific training effect will take place.

Trajectory: the path or flight pattern of an object moving through the air.

Trend: the latest and most popular attraction or activity.

Trunk: the middle part of your body (midsection).

U

Urban areas: geographical areas consisting of towns or cities.

User groups: particular groups of people who use leisure facilities.

United Kingdom Coaching

Certificate (UKCC): a government-led initiative that is an endorsement of a sport-specific coach education programme.

Vocation: a regular occupation for which you would be particularly qualified or suited.

Whole-school approach: something that is an essential part of everything a school does.

Index